THROUGH THEIR EYES

Bible stories told by
the women who were there

Gina Bolton

Emily B.

ISBN: 1534716106
ISBN 13: 9781534716100
Library of Congress Control Number: 2016910403
CreateSpace Independent Publishing Platform
North Charleston, South Carolina

About the cover

The art displayed on the cover of this book is not only beautiful but also unique. It was created by Doug Powell who uses puzzle pieces to fashion his amazing art. When I saw the image online, I knew it was the one I wanted for the cover of the book. I immediately emailed Mr. Powell and asked about the possibility of using it. He was gracious enough to allow me to do so. The more I thought about the way the image was created, the more I realized how perfect it was for this project. Each of us is like Doug's beautiful work; we are created from many different "puzzle pieces". Sometimes it is difficult to see how God is using each piece to make us into something beautiful. But when the image is all put together, what emerges is a rich tapestry of complexity — obviously designed by a purposeful artist. The stories of the women in this book are like that, too. Each one is a puzzle piece that tells another part of God's story and reveals another aspect of His character. My prayer is that you will be able to see God clearly by the end of this book. The puzzle will be complete. And in seeing God through the eyes of the women of this book, you will understand with a new freshness how much He loves you.

Table of Contents

Introduction

The idea for this book came into being a few years ago when I was helping to plan a women's retreat with another church. Our theme for the weekend was *Beautiful In God's Eyes*. As women, we seem to have so many issues around our appearance. While we may blame outside forces for these feelings, many of these pressures come from within us. As I thought about what it meant to be a woman of beauty, I remembered the three most beautiful women I had ever known. Not one of them would have won a beauty contest or even been considered a candidate. Not one of them had wealth or power as the world sees those attributes. But they all had an inner beauty of spirit that drew people to them. They possessed a wealth of love and peace that the world doesn't often understand. They had power to live at peace with their situation in life and be content. These three women all loved God with a devotion that I did not even see in my local parish priest. These are the qualities of beauty that do not fade away with age, gray hair, and wrinkles. In the Bible, Peter lifts up the value of a quiet and gentle spirit, and these women all captured that essence.

My relationship with these three deeply spiritual women led me to wonder how the women of the Bible experienced the events that are recorded. Most of the stories are told from a man's perspective, but I wondered what the women saw, felt, and thought. What was the impact on the women who witnessed all of the tragedies and triumphs?

Let me take a moment to give some background. I grew up on a Caribbean island, on a sugar cane plantation. My family lived on the second floor of the Great House; my grandfather lived on the first floor with his second wife and their daughter. It was a wonderful place to grow up in many ways. I have memories of skipping through fields, climbing trees, building tree houses, and having picnics in the branches of the guava trees. I remember that a couple of times a week, the bread man would drive onto the plantation and deliver the freshly baked bread. He had these delicious cakes with pink icing that I loved. When he opened the back doors of his truck, the smell of fresh bread filled my tiny nose.

We had a huge vegetable garden with all kinds of wonderful snacks for a young girl. Any time I was hungry, all I had to do was go into the garden, pull up a carrot or pick a tomato, wash it over the giant witch's cauldron that caught the water from the faucet, and munch away. My siblings, cousins, and I also loved to walk barefoot in that garden after it rained and see who could get the thickest mud shoes on their feet. When I remember the warm, wet mud squishing up between my toes, I can feel the delight even today. Isn't it great what kids can enjoy?

As a child, I had a nanny named Duggie. She helped to care for my siblings and me. Duggie was quite elderly. I knew she was old because she had gray hair, I could outrun her, and she had absolutely no teeth. Every time we made her laugh, she would put her hand in front of her mouth so that we could not see her gums. The night after Duggie died, I had a dream about her. In the dream, she was running in a lovely, green field, and she was laughing. She had teeth. That was when I knew she was in heaven.

She had been my mother's nanny years earlier, so she was really a part of our family. She was like a beloved grandmother. One of my fondest memories of Duggie is of her sitting with me at bedtime, rubbing my aching legs, and singing songs to me as I fell asleep.

Our housemaid, Brown, was the second woman who left a deep imprint on my life. She was quiet and caring. Any time I think of her, I remember her smile. Unlike Duggie, she did have all of her teeth. She was not only a wonderful cook, but she could bake the most amazing cakes. Sometimes she would allow me to help her, especially with the icing. I loved to lick the bowl.

I always knew I was safe when I was with Duggie or Brown. They often protected me during some difficult times in my childhood. Many times they put my wants and desires above their own. To put it very simply, they loved me even when I was not so loveable and even when it cost them a great deal.

Duggie and Browne often shared with me how much God loved them, and their love for Him. All of their actions were motivated by love. Even though they had little wealth, power, and possessions, they were happy. As a young child, I noticed the difference in them. There is great beauty in contentment.

The third woman who radiated true beauty was a complete stranger named Gwen. She was from the island but had moved away as a young woman to work in New York. She returned to the island each year at Christmas to visit family. One Christmas, she attended a school play in which I was cast as the main character, Puss In Boots. Gwen told me she fell in love with me during the show. Afterwards, she came backstage and introduced herself to my family. I was ten years old. As strange as it may seem, she adopted me as a part of her family, and from that time forward wrote letters to me, often sending along prayers and encouragement. Gwen always talked about how wonderful God had been to her throughout her life. She asked nothing in return for her love, just as Brown and Duggie did not. They simply loved me unconditionally.

In planning for the retreat, I was thinking about what makes a woman beautiful. I immediately thought of these three women. In those moments, I realized that I had never really considered their profound impact on my life. Without them, I would not be who I am today. Simply said, they brought beauty into my life. That is one of the things God has created women to do, to share their beauty with the world. As the retreat loomed, I wrote a couple of short dramas retelling well-known Bible stories. I wanted all of us to see those stories through the eyes of women who were there.

That was the beginning of this book. The events in each chapter are from the Bible, but I have taken some liberties and added information that while culturally accurate, is fictional. I invite you to read and listen to these stories as if you were sitting with these women, having coffee, and chatting. You will notice that in a historical time period when women were considered less important than men and had no rights to speak of, God honored them and used them to spread His most important message.

My prayer is that as you read these stories, you will understand God's love for you. You will see how very beautiful you are in His eyes. You will recognize the beauty that is within you, the beauty God wants you to share with the world. You will feel His great love for you and be transformed.

1

Eve

Most of you know my story quite well. It is probably a story that can be told from memory. Even though you might know the facts, I want to tell you the story from my perspective. Don't worry; I won't try to shrug off all of the blame. I have learned my lesson. I just want to share my experience with you in hopes that you can learn something from my mistakes. Maybe you will be able to see clearly through my eyes.

Many of you know me as Eve, the very first woman, shaped by the hands of God. Talk about being fearfully and wonderfully made. I will forever remember opening my eyes for the first time and looking into the most amazing face, the face of God. His face was radiant, and simply looking at Him was satisfying. I immediately felt whole, loved, content. When He took me by the hand and led me to Adam, there was an instant connection between us. We were able to communicate even without speaking. It was what every woman since has wanted: a man who is able to read her mind.

Later, Adam would describe for me his own awakening and the naming of all the creatures who shared the garden with us. As God brought each animal to Adam to name, Adam claimed that he looked for one who shared a special connection with him. But not one was found. Finally, God caused a deep sleepiness to close Adam's eyes, and while he slept peacefully, God took one of his ribs and fashioned the perfect mate, friend, partner for Adam: me.

God was pleased with me and with the union between Adam and me. God saw all He had made and proclaimed that it was very good. We lived in complete harmony in the perfect garden God created for us. Eden was a place of unique beauty and peace. Even now, I do not have the words to successfully describe what life there was like. Trying to do so would leave me feeling inadequate, as I could only give you such a small and shadowy vision of Eden that it would be futile to even try. Believe me when I say it was the perfect place in all ways. I never stopped longing to return there throughout my entire life on Earth.

We also had perfect communion with God. We could walk and talk with Him daily without any hiding or shame.

Shame came later.

Even to this day, I cannot think what brought me to the place of doubt that led me to go against what God had told me. I loved Adam, and I loved God. I thought I loved them both with all of my heart. Life seemed so simple and pure back then, until the day I decided to trust my feelings more than I trusted God.

That fateful day, I was sitting by a crystal, bubbling river, talking with some of the water creatures, when I noticed the serpent just across the riverbank. We did not see him very often. In fact it was a rare occurrence. As I looked at him, I experienced a strange desire to go the center of the garden. That was the area where the one tree from which we were not allowed to eat stood. It was certainly a grand tree, beautiful to look at, and it offered pleasant shade for us and the other animals who wanted to rest beneath its magnificent branches. In many ways, it was not really much different than the other trees in Eden. I cannot say that I had ever before that day focused specifically on this tree. I had simply taken God at His word when He said not to eat its fruit. I do not even remember contemplating the second part of God's warning.

On the day that you eat of it, you will surely die.

Death was not something that was a part of Eden living. I had never before thought about what it was or about the real impact death would have on me. It was a completely foreign concept to me. God wanted it to stay that way. He did not want us to deal with the burden that death would bring into our lives and ultimately into the world itself.

On this particular day, I felt compelled to seek out this tree. I rose quickly and started toward the center of the garden. My thinking was focused completely on reaching that tree. My first mistake was in not taking the time to pause and think about what exactly I was doing. I simply responded to feelings. As I hurried toward the tree, Adam saw me and followed quietly. I did not stop to wait for him, as I would normally have done. I wanted to be ahead of him. He did not hasten to catch up with me. This was very unusual for us. Adam and I were one unit. We shared all of life together in the fullest sense possible. There was perfect communion between us. We had never experienced the doubt that happens in all relationships today. We never wondered if one of us was displeased with the other. That is why it is so difficult to explain or understand why I did what I did next. It was as if the more I hurried toward the tree, the farther away from Adam I drew, and not only physically. I just yearned to be near that tree.

As the tree of the knowledge of good and evil came into sight, I felt a kind of nervous excitement and intrigue that I had not experienced before. I remember thinking that I was glad Adam was not at my side as he usually was. My skin tingled as I stood beneath the shady branches and noticed the luscious-looking fruit that seemed to be dripping from the gracious limbs just overhead. My brain was warning me to remember what God had lovingly told us about the fruit of that tree. I could almost hear God's voice whisper, "Remember how much I love you." But somehow when the serpent approached and started to question me about what God had said, I did not tell the simple truth. I exaggerated.

Let me explain about the serpent. I know that many of you immediately think of slimy, scaly creatures when you think of serpents. You may recoil at the name of this creature. You may wonder why I did not run screaming away as soon as I saw this snake in the grass. But the creature you envision is not the way he once was. The serpent was one of the most beautiful creatures in all of Eden. On the rare occasion that Adam and I saw him across the garden, we would immediately stop whatever we were doing and focus completely on him. His coloring and movements were compelling in a way that not even the graceful giraffes were. His skin was almost luminous. Until this day, he had never approached either of us. There were at least two other facts about him that should have caused me to pause and consider his suggestions that day. First, he was unusual in that he alone did not have a mate as all of the other creatures in Eden did. Second, he was never near when God walked in the garden with us.

All of creation in Eden praised the Creator. When sitting by the river, I noticed that the rushing water sang a song of praise to God. Each droplet joined in a chorus as it leapt and flowed downstream. The flowers that opened their fragile petals each morning, awakened with such loveliness, they thanked God for their very existence. I guess I should try to explain that in Eden, there was so much more to communication than what is known today. We did not always speak to communicate. It was often more like what today is called intuition. So, even though I could not hear with my ears the language of the flowers and the trees or even the water, my spirit could understand what was being communicated. I am sure this sounds rather unusual. After that day, when everything changed, and we had to leave Eden, this was one of the things I missed the most. We never again were able to hear the voices of the water, flowers, sky, or earth praising God in their own languages.

But let me get back to the serpent. I did not realize until much later that not only was the serpent never present when God was, but he was the one creature who never praised the Creator. Why did I not notice these things before?

As I stood beneath those branches, experiencing this strange yearning, the beautiful, crafty serpent slithered into my personal space. I moved my lips to object, but the yearning grew stronger within me. I did not utter a word. Adam stood not too far away, and he remained silent, also. For the first time, I felt a slight separation from him. Before my mind could fully take this in, the serpent moved closer still. His colorful body shone so brightly that I felt hypnotized by the rainbow of shimmering colors reflected on the broad leaves of the tree. My senses were overwhelmed by the sight and also by the sweet aroma that filled my nostrils. At the time, I thought it must be the luscious fruit, but later, the fruit never again had such an enticing scent. Could that smell have been from the serpent himself? My senses were on overload. I felt so full that I simply had to groan aloud with happiness. Even though I say I felt full, my body and emotions screamed for something more. I did not know what that *more* could or should be.

All of this happened before that serpent even opened his smiling mouth and spoke his first word. As my spirit clamored for that something more, the silky, smooth voice of the serpent spoke to my need.

"Has God really said you must not eat of this, the most pleasing and satisfying fruit in all of the garden?" His words were like little flames that stoked the fire of want growing stronger and hotter in my soul. I was panting with a burning desire that was completely new to me and was shaking me: body, mind, and spirit.

I could hardly form the words that I whispered in response. I knew I was exaggerating what God had told us when I said, "We are not to eat this fruit or even touch it lest we die."

Laughter, lusty and contagious, broke forth from that hypnotizing mouth. Softly and convincingly he whispered into my ear, so close that his breath brought pleasure bumps on my neck and arms, "You surely will not die. God Himself knows that when you bite into this exquisite fruit, you will become like Him. You will know all things. He has not been completely honest with you. Do you not feel a deep longing for something more? Do your senses not tell you that they need more in this instant? Are you not, even now, experiencing a delicious feeling that you have never felt before?"

I will never be certain, but I do believe that those questions were sealed into my consciousness with a kiss. His lips brushed my ear and neck. A ripple of longing ran from my neck to my toes. I held my breath.

There was silence all around me. If my brain had been functioning clearly, I would have known that something was terribly wrong.

Eden was a peaceful place, but as I have said before, the earth, every part of it, filled the air with the praises of God. In those moments, not a song from bird, or flower, or animal could be heard. I did not think about Adam for a moment. He did not say a word to me. In all of the years after, we have never spoken of that moment.

Before I could process those provocative words or hardly blink, the serpent was holding a ripe piece of fruit a mere whisper away from my lips. All of the yearning I was feeling centered on that one object.

"Just one bite and you will find the satisfaction you are longing for. One bite and you will know all things as God does. You will be a god. Follow this need that is so strong in you. Enjoy the beauty around you. Enjoy this feeling."

His voice was so seductive. My mouth was watering, as my heart was thundering in my breast. I could not take my eyes off that piece of fruit and the serpent's mouth just beside it. He seemed about ready to lick the colorful skin. I did not even need to reach for that prize as the serpent lifted my willing hand and placed it into my fingers.

"Taste and see for yourself. Do not resist this feeling. It is good, so good."

I wish I could tell you that I did not know what I was doing. But I did. I knew in my heart that what I was about to do would go directly against what God had commanded. I just did not take the time to care, to think about consequences, to reason through the decision. I wanted the satisfaction that the serpent offered. I wanted to be like God. I wanted to do this before Adam could. I wanted to choose against God.

My lips opened and rested softly on the delicacy. I bit into it, and the juice trickled down my chin. The serpent began laughing again, softly at first. The yearning deep inside of me vanished before I was even able to enjoy the sweet taste of that bite. I slowly opened my eyes and looked at the serpent. Where had those overwhelming desires gone? I was left feeling empty.

Soft laughter grew into a twisted and vicious sound. It was completely different than his earlier laughter. It made me feel threatened. I looked around for Adam. I needed him. My mind screamed for him. The serpent's laughter grew more violent. I was startled and screamed when Adam's hand touched my shoulder. A new feeling was growing inside of me. The yearning was replaced by what I know now as regret. My body felt fatigued suddenly. The weight of regret felt so heavy on my chest that I could not catch my breath. I looked into Adam's face, but found I could not look him in the eye. Something was wrong.

Adam was focused on the bitten fruit in my hand. His eyes were fixed on it. I felt angry with him. Where had he been when I needed him? He had not spoken a single word throughout my entire exchange with that snake. Why didn't he help me to resist?

The serpent became quiet. All of Eden waited.

I lifted the fruit up to Adam's mouth as his eyes feasted on its pulpy flesh. He raised his eyes to mine for a brief moment. I nodded, and he leaned in and bit into the tantalizing fruit. His eyes closed in ecstasy.

Silence.

Then an explosion of noise erupted around us. It was discordant shouting, cursing, and bawdy laughter rolled into one. I realized it was coming from the serpent that had transformed. He no longer appeared beautiful at all. The glorious scent, which moments before had surrounded me, was gone. Now an overly-sweet stench filled my nostrils. The harsh chorus emanating from the serpent was accompanied by another sound I had never heard before. It tore at my soul. Another new feeling entered my awareness, sorrow. These sounds pierced the silence of the garden, and I was forced to cover my ears with my hands that were still sticky from the nectar.

I could not communicate with Adam. Our thoughts were not able to connect as they had always done in the past. I sank to my knees there beneath the tree. Adam fell to my left.

I do not really know how long we stayed like that, hands over our ears. After what seemed like a lifetime, I noticed only one sound, sorrowful moaning. The laughter had ended. Slowly, I lowered my hands. Adam did the same. The serpent was gone. We glanced at each other and looked away immediately. Adam's face had changed. Did he see a change in mine as well? Oh, there were certainly changes inside my soul, awful changes. There was an entirely new and disturbing set of feelings that I had never before experienced: doubt, fear, guilt, shame, separation. It was devastating.

My hands went from my ears to my body. Another first for me, I wanted to hide from my partner. I had never known nakedness before. Now, I felt horribly exposed. I felt uncomfortable with my nakedness before Adam. I used my hands to cover myself. They were not enough. I reached out for some broad leaves from a nearby bush. Even with the green covering, I felt so vulnerable. I wanted Adam to stop looking at me. I could feel disgust and anger growing like weeds in me. Ugly words started to fill my mind. I no longer felt a unity with Adam. What had happened to me, to us?

Can you even believe the fig leaf clothing? What a pitiful idea. If it wasn't so deadly serious, it would be so very funny. Leaves do not make great clothing.

As we stood there silently accusing each other, I realized that the groaning and weeping that I still heard was coming from creation around us. As I glanced around, the garden looked as though it had faded in its vibrancy. The water flowed more sluggishly in the river, and the trees looked different, old? All of these words were new to my vocabulary back then. I could not name them in my mind at the time, but I learned very quickly their meaning in the hours and days after my serpent encounter.

When I chanced another look at Adam, I realized that his face was wet. I touched my own cheeks. Tears were flowing freely down my face as well. Some of the groans that I heard were ours.

Now, when we looked at each other, we did not see only love and acceptance; there was doubt, judgment, and distrust. Both Adam and I were unsure of what to do. We started to run away from that tree as fast as we could. However, we could not outrun the awful sadness and feelings of loss that invaded us. I stopped running only when my lungs could not gasp another breath. Adam collapsed just ahead of me.

We had often run through Eden enjoying both the pleasure it brought to us, and the vista around us. Even the animals would sometimes join with us, running and leaping simply for the joy of it. This time we were trying to outrun the sound of sorrow groaning in the air and the wretchedness we were both feeling. As we lay panting on the ground, we heard God's voice calling. A great fear came upon us. We were naked and would have to go before God and try to explain what was happening in Eden. How could we do this?

Why did I listen to my feelings? Why did I doubt what my loving Father had told me? Why did I choose to listen to the crafty serpent, to follow my own desires?

Believe me when I say, I have searched my brain to try to come up with answers to these questions. I don't have any, not satisfying ones, anyway. What I can say is that in those moments, the serpent's suggestions made a lot of sense. He was definitely crafty. His voice was smooth, and he was flattering. He made everything sound so perfect, and made God seem petty in His restrictions. However, I chose to go against what my loving God had told me. It was my choice.

Maybe you can understand how I felt in those moments. Perhaps you have had a similar experience when you were standing on the edge of a decision, trying to follow your conscience but being overwhelmed by your feelings. In that moment, my feelings were so strong and pulled in what seemed like the right direction at the time. The serpent's words appeared to be so logical, so right. My heart wanted it all to be true even as my mind was screaming against the choice. I chose to listen to the wrong voice. It was my decision. I could claim that the serpent made me do it, but I would be lying to you. He only offered. If I had taken the time to think, to remember God, to connect with Adam, even to listen to the voices of Eden around me, I would have known this was wrong. I knew I was choosing against God in that moment. I am the only one to blame.

Of course, you know that I did not immediately accept the blame when God asked what I had done. I blamed the serpent. How quickly my relationship with God went from trust and unity to doubt, accusation, and discord.

When God called to us in the garden, we were shaking with fear. Adam waited for me to answer. I was so terrified; I could not utter a single sound. I did not think I could stand in front of God without crumbling into dust at His feet. Finally, Adam answered God's call. "I hear you calling, but I have hidden since I am naked."

"Who told you that you are naked? Have you eaten from the forbidden tree?"

Obviously, God knew what we had done. He knows all things, but He was giving Adam a chance to confess his wrongdoing. Adam did not do that. He decided to blame me for giving him the fruit and even went further by trying to blame God for bringing me into the garden in the first place.

"The woman whom You gave to be with me, she gave me from the tree, and I ate."

You must know, in that moment I wanted to grab the biggest tree limb I could swing and clobber that stupid man over the head. Honestly, I was furious with Adam.

However, when God turned his attention to me, I did not perform any better. Although, at the time I felt quite superior to Adam as I did not throw any blame his way. But oh, how I wanted to. I thought God would be happy with my response.

"The serpent deceived me and I ate."

Most certainly, I was deceived but not just by the serpent. I was deceiving myself and was not willing to admit it.

God could not be fooled then, and He cannot be fooled now. He knows what is going on in our hearts even when we may not realize it ourselves. He could see right through my false humility and see what I was trying to do. He did not accept either explanation. The consequences for our choices were shattering.

God said that eating the fruit would bring death, and it certainly did. There were a thousand deaths before our physical deaths: the death of our relationship with each other, with the other creatures, with Eden, and all of creation, and finally with God. We had to leave Eden. No longer did we have a perfect life. No longer could we have intimate interaction daily with God in the garden. No longer could we communicate with the trees, flowers, rivers, or animals. No longer could Adam and

I communicate with each other without misunderstanding and doubt. We lost so much. We could not have survived without the help that God provided for us. Even though we had turned away from His offer of relationship, He continued to take care of us. He did have to send us out of the garden, which was awful. However, He continued to communicate with us even though it was not the way it used to be. How could it be? Even though God had not changed, Adam and I had changed completely.

What I hope you can see is how easy it is to be enticed and carried away by our own desires. We often do not pause and think about the fact that every good and perfect gift comes to us from God. He does not withhold good things from us. He is our loving Father and will give us all things necessary for life and godliness. He wants us to experience abundant life and live it to the fullest. We ought never to doubt His goodness or His word.

When that happens and our feelings start to crowd out clear thinking, we should pause and ask God for His help.

We should once again listen to the sounds and sights of creation all around us as they praise God for the beauty of His world.

We ought to call for our friends and ask them to help us remember the words of our loving Father so that we are not deceived into making choices that will most certainly bring pain and isolation into our lives.

It does seem to be very human to justify and blame when we make poor choices in life. It takes enormous courage to humbly admit our guilt and confess it openly without any *buts*. Believe me, I know how difficult that is. It is a lesson I continued to relearn throughout my life.

One thing I want you to remember is that God is a God of second chances, or maybe I should say, many chances. Even when we are not completely honest with Him, He is willing to forgive and help us back onto the path toward wholeness.

His love never fails.

His patience is remarkable.

His sacrifice for us is the first and truest of all legends.

2

Ahlam

This is going to be a whale of a tale. I'm sorry, but I just had to say that, even knowing that you will sigh and call me childish. I think you will recognize the story I have to tell. You have heard it many times, and many of you may have doubted that it could actually have happened. You have tried to explain it by saying that perhaps it is just a fanciful tale meant to teach a real lesson. You are partially right. It is definitely meant to teach a lesson. But you are wrong on the other part. Trust me. It happened. It almost caused me to suffer a heat attack. It was assuredly the most terrifying moment of my life.

Allow me to start at the very beginning. My name is Ahlam. I lived in the city of Nineveh. This was one of the greatest cities in the world, the capital city of Assyria. In many ways it was a wonderful city in which to live. Because it was such a wealthy city, one could enjoy all of the good things in life. We were a very progressive city for our time. We had temples for many gods in our city with the main temple built for the worship of the goddess Ishtar. She was a fertility goddess, and so there were many temple priestesses. I was not supposed to know exactly what went on in the temples of Ishtar, but I did. My mother would have been horrified to know what I knew. But you see, I had good ears. I had learned to listen very carefully when the adults were speaking. They often ignored me because I was just a young girl. That was fine with me as it allowed me to listen in on many interesting conversations. My friend Anthony often teased me about my big ears. Well, those big ears had allowed me to learn many intriguing things.

The worship practices in the temple of Ishtar along with child sacrifices to the different gods were considered quite normal for us. No one gave these practices a second thought.

We were also a military power, and so we were respected and feared throughout the ancient world. No one would consider trying to invade our city. They would surely fail in their attempt. We felt very safe in our city since the walls surrounding us stood at least fifteen feet high. Just calling myself a Ninevite made me feel quite superior. I had been born in this city and had lived my entire life here so far.

Our king built the most beautiful palace ever constructed. I had never been inside the walls, of course, but I heard that it boasted over 80 rooms. Since I was very good at eavesdropping, I knew that the king called it a "palace without parallel." My family was quite wealthy, but we did not have even half that many rooms in our house. I certainly would have loved to explore inside the palace. I heard that there were all kinds of treasures within, including wondrous gardens designed and built for the king. There were many times when I daydreamed about being invited to the palace and given a tour by the king himself. I decided that I would only allow my parents to come on the tour with me if they had not taken away any of my privileges for at least a week. Since that never happened, I did not really think that they would join me on the royal tour.

Our city was planned well with canals and aqueducts to water the parks and gardens that all citizens were free to enjoy. We were a learned city, too. There were many beautiful structures where the philosophers would gather to discuss their lofty ideas. I did try to eavesdrop on their conversations a few times, but I could not quite understand what they were discussing.

We were free to enjoy a good life and not worry about any kind of disaster. How could any of our leaders have known that we were heading down a path of destruction? We were about to come face to face with someone who would tell us exactly what would happen to us if we did not repent of our wickedness.

Now, Nineveh was a city on the Tigris River. We were a place of commerce as we basically connected the Mediterranean Sea with the Indian Ocean. The river was the life-blood of our city in many ways. It was out of this very river that our warning came.

I had always been drawn to the water, even as a very young girl. I enjoyed walking along the banks of the river, sometimes in the early morning or at sunset. I knew certain places where I could be completely alone, where there were the best rocks for skipping, and where I could wade into the water up to my waist and cool off on a hot day. I found it quite peaceful and relished the quiet that could be found at some points along the flowing water.

I was in for a big surprise one unforgettable day as I strolled along enjoying some thinking time. I recall thinking about an especially wonderful meal that had been served at dinner the night before. The bread had been quite unusual, and I was desperate to know what our slave had done differently to make it so sweet and chewy. Unfortunately, my mother did not want me to talk to the cook. She thought that was beneath my station in life. She thought I should spend my days doing *other things*. She never really explained to me what those *other things* should be.

Everything that interested me was unacceptable to my mother. I was somewhat of a disappointment to her. I know that my actions were the main reason she sighed so much. I did not really try to upset her. It just seemed to happen, often. But can you really blame me? My name means witty, imaginative, and one who has pleasant dreams. When my mother shook her head and called me a dreamer, I took it as a compliment. But I do not think she meant it as one. Even in my best dreams, I could not have created such a fantastic story as what I am about to tell.

As I walked along the pebbly shore that day, I bent down to avoid a low-hanging tree branch, and heard a rushing sound. I looked out over the water of the mighty river. A rather large wave was crashing in my direction. I scrambled back several steps knocking my head hard against the tree branch as the wall of water rushed up onto the bank. Just as I was wondering if I should hoist my skirts and climb the tree at my back, a huge sea monster's head emerged from the murky water. I noticed its eyes were almost black and the size of the large pot used to collect rainwater in the courtyard of my home. The monster itself was dark in color, with the largest, most hideous mouth imaginable. I felt as though it could not only swallow me whole, but also consume the tree behind me with one gulp. As I pressed myself against the tree, the fish shook its head violently, contorted its rubbery-looking body, and spit something enormous onto the ground just a short distance away from my now completely drenched feet. I closed my eyes and started screaming.

I thought for sure that the gods had decided to come and take me away for some slight I had caused them. I never really was a very religious young girl. I was not sure what all the fuss was about with all of the religions our city played at following. They appeared to be designed to entertain or to make money for the merchants. These men were always creating some new trinket to sell that would honor Ishtar or one of the other lesser gods. There were the idols that were supposed to protect your house, your belongings, your life, anything and everything imaginable. My family, alone, must have owned one of each of the idols ever created in our fine city. My mother loved to show off the room where she kept the large stone idols and several smaller metal idols that had cost her many silver pieces. Since I often played around the idols as a young girl, I had seen the disrespect many of the slaves had for them. When they were supposed to be dusting the statues, they would say rude things to them, bump them, and even kick them. I found that last offense quite silly, as the kicker would usually walk away from the encounter limping. Anyway, if these statues were really gods who were protecting us, shouldn't they have been able to first protect themselves? Wouldn't they have been angry with these slaves? Wouldn't they have punished them in some way?

Sorry, I am off-track again with my story.

There I was, wet to the waist, smelling like river water, screaming my lungs out, waiting to be eaten by the sea monster, or carted off to the Underworld for some terrible offense I had committed against one of the hundreds of gods my mother tried to teach me about. After a few moments, I realized that nothing was attacking. I gingerly opened my eyes a crack and peered around for whatever danger was near. The terrifying water monster had disappeared. I opened my eyes fully. Of course the gods were not coming to get me. The monster was gone, and I now had an amazing story to tell my friend, Basilah. She loved my stories.

I was about to take a tentative step away from the tree when I heard moaning. I screamed again. I looked around wondering if another monster was approaching. What I saw next was almost as hideous as the large fish. Out of the mud and silt along the riverbank, a figure slowly rose. It was the blob that the hideous creature had spit out. I wanted to run away but was frozen in place. My feet would not obey the orders my brain was sending to flee.

The extremely pale figure continued to moan and started to wave its arms around. It was coming towards me when it tripped and fell back into the water. Was it a water creature? It was submerged for quite a while. Suddenly, its head appeared above the water. It was a human head, a man's face, but quite ugly. The hair on his head was white as the flour used for our bread and so was his skin. As he rose unsteadily from the water, I could not help but notice that everything on this man's body was white. From the top of his head to his bony feet, he was ghostly white. His tattered robe was white. Never in all of my life had I seen anything like this. He was the large blob the river monster had vomited onto the rocky beach.

He looked about as bizarre as any of the strange animals I had seen in the market. These animals were brought by boat from faraway lands, and sold to wealthy, bored men for pets. This was not going to be anyone's pet. He was too horrible to look upon. He started to speak and wave his arms in the air again. It took all of my courage to walk closer to him and ask if he needed my help. He most certainly needed someone's help, and as my nose could tell, he desperately needed a bath.

He had just been coughed up onto the beach by a very large fish. That meant he had been alive inside its belly. This was amazing. I had so many questions I wanted to ask him. However before he was able to tell me anything, he was going to need some attention. He did not seem able to do more than moan and groan in response to my offer of help. I was able to wrap one of his arms around my shoulders and begin what would be a very long walk back to my house. The stranger was barely able to drag his feet all the while groaning and babbling like a crazy man. This took a great deal of effort on my part as I am not what anyone might call a strong girl and because he smelled like fish that had been sitting out in the sun for too long. I do not know how I did not do what the river monster had recently done and cough up my breakfast.

However, I was so eager to get my questions answered, that I hauled him as far as I could. I am sorry to say, it was not too far before my energy was spent. We still had quite a long walk to get to my home. I also did not want an adult to come along and take this man away from me before I got the chance to speak with him. If an adult passed by and saw us, I knew he would end up in someone else's home. I decided to stash him safely in one of my hiding places near some bushes, run home, get one of the house slaves I could trust not to blab to my mother or father, and come back for the fish man. Happily, my plan worked. The fishy-smelling man was so feverish that I don't think he knew what was going on around him. I really hoped he would remember something of being inside that monster fish.

It took two very long and boring days of staying inside and caring for Fish Man, my name for him, before he finally opened his eyes and was able to look at me calmly. He did still look a bit confused, but I could tell the fever had broken. I started to tell him where he was and that he was safe for now. Before I could get very far, he interrupted.

"Am I really in Nineveh?" His voice sounded hoarse and rusty like it had not been used in a while.

"Yes, you are in our glorious city. Welcome to..."

Again he interrupted me with what sounded like a curse. I could not be completely sure as he was speaking a dialect with which I was not completely familiar. He certainly did not seem very happy to be here or to be alive. It did not look like he was going to be grateful to me for saving his life. I had practiced a lovely, humble speech to explain to him how I had single-handedly rescued him from the enormous fish. Okay, perhaps I had exaggerated a bit. But I had brought him home and nursed him back to health. Shouldn't he be somewhat grateful?

Fish Man tried to get up from his mat and stand. He was not too successful.

"I think you need a few more days of rest before you are ready for walking or trying to return to your home, wherever that is," I said. All I got in response was a sigh. Did all adults sigh when children tried to help and offer suggestions or opinions about life?

The hours of waiting around inside the house were difficult for me. I had not spent this much time inside my house since I was five years old and suffered from some awful fever. Another day dragged by before Fish Man was ready to stand on his own without help. He walked around the room, and then stopped right in front of me.

"What is your name girl?"

"Ahlam," I answered quickly. "I was by the river when the giant monster spit you up onto the rocks. I was terrified and might even have screamed a little, but not much. You were inside its belly. I have waited for three days to ask you a million questions. Like what happened that you ended up being swallowed by such a monster, and how long were you inside, and what was that like, and were there other creatures in there with you, and why are you as white as the wool on our sheep, and how did you breathe...."

Before I could finish my questions, Fish Man growled. He is definitely the first human I have heard growl. He stomped away and started muttering to himself; at least I do not think he was talking to me as he was using his dialect again. At one point he shook his fist in the air. He had obviously been hurt in his head while inside the smelly belly. If he continued to raise his voice, my mother might hear the noise and decide to come to investigate. I guess she was due for a visit as I had not seen her for four days now. Usually, she would see me as least once every three or four days.

Fish Man settled down on his mat on the floor as if his legs would no longer hold him. Suddenly, he laughed softly and shook his head.

"So you want to hear my story, girl?"

"I should like nothing better, Fish..er, sir," I replied. "And my name is Ahlam."

"Well, I will tell you my story. And then I will have to tell the whole city. But I do not think I am strong enough for that yet, so I will start with you. My name is Jonah. I am a prophet sent to Nineveh by God to bring the city a message."

"Which god sent you here. I do not know of a god who uses sea monsters," I laughed.

"If you wish to hear my story, you will have to hold your tongue, girl," he grumbled.

"Okay, Fish Man," I muttered under my breath. He glared at me, and I put my best smile on my face. "I will listen quietly."

"Well, we shall see about that." He rubbed a pale hand over his face and then stared at its whiteness for several seconds before shaking his head and settling into a comfortable position.

"I see that my time inside that monster has changed my appearance quite a bit. I wonder if my friends and family will recognize me when I return home?"

"I am certain they will be quite surprised at first. But do not worry about that now. Tell me how you ended up inside that enormous, vicious monster in the first place."

Fish Man chuckled before answering. "I had forgotten how impatient the young can be. I will start at the beginning and try to satisfy your curiosity. It is true that I am a prophet of Yahweh, the God of Israel. He is the only true God. He is mighty and a righteous judge. But I have learned very recently, in some very unusual ways, that He is also a merciful God. Much more merciful than I want Him to be."

Oh no, this was going to be a religious story, and they were my least favorite. I guess old Jonah saw the disgust on my face because he chuckled again and continued.

"I know you are anxious to get your questions answered, but this is my story. I must tell it from the beginning. That is the only way to bring this message to you."

I nodded my head and prepared to be bored. I hoped that the good part would not come too close to the end of the story.

Fish Man continued. "God came to me one day, not too long ago, and told me to come to this very city. He wanted me to bring a message to your people. He is greatly displeased with all of you. He sees the awful wickedness of Nineveh day and night. He commands you to repent. I did not want to do what He said. I knew that if I came to Nineveh with God's message, then the people might repent and turn to God. I did not want that to happen. I would rather have God destroy this entire evil city."

I could not believe what he said. Did he realize that he was talking to one of the people living right here in the very city he wanted his God to destroy? I stared at him with fear. Maybe I should have left him on the bank of the river, covered in mud, and moaning with his fever. There was a long silence as we looked at each other. I guess he was realizing that one of the people he hated had helped to save his life. He looked down at his pasty hands.

"I may be a prophet, but I am not perfect. I will just continue my story now." He cleared his throat and continued. "I decided to run in the opposite direction. I found a boat that was heading for Joppa and boarded. I thought I could run away from Almighty God that easily. But, once again, I underestimated Jehovah. He sent a fierce storm that threatened to sink the ship. The sailors worked as hard as they could to keep the boat from sinking. Everyone on board was praying to his own god, asking for help. I was asleep below deck when the captain awakened me and asked that I call on my God and see if He could help with the storm. Immediately, I knew the reason for the storm. God was getting my attention. I still had such a hard heart, that I would rather die than come to Nineveh. I told the captain that the storm was my fault. If he wanted to save his ship, he would have to throw me into the sea."

I could not stop myself from gasping at this point. How very much this man hated our city. He would rather die than come to give us a message from his God.

"What happened next?" I whispered.

"Well, that is just what the captain did. He had a couple of his strongest sailors throw me overboard into that black, roiling sea. I cannot say I was not scared. I started saying my prayers, wondering if God would hear me since I was disobeying Him. I was swallowing mouthfuls of seawater and could not keep my head above the water. The waves were crashing over my head. Suddenly, out of the deep, a huge shadow moved toward me. The next thing I knew, I was sliding past large teeth, down a slippery gullet. It was so very hot inside the fish's stomach. I felt as though I could not breath, and I began to panic. I must have lost consciousness as I don't remember too much except that I would occasionally awaken from my stupor and realize it was not a dream. I guess eventually the thing brought me to the shores of Nineveh just as God wanted."

Fish Man stopped talking. I waited. This was not a very satisfying story. Didn't he understand how to describe things in such a way as to make a story interesting? This should have been the best story ever, and it was as dull as my mother's conversations.

So Fish Man could not remember any details of being inside the belly of the monster and could not answer any of my questions. It was so frustrating. Believe me when I tell you I asked him several times about his experience. What he did want to talk about was this God of his, the God of the Israelites. I did not know much about Jehovah, as Fish Man called him. I asked a lot of questions about Him. Fish Man turned out to be a great storyteller after all when telling me stories about Jehovah.

He told me about how his God created the world, how He chose the Israelites as His people, how He rescued them from Egypt and slavery and gave them a new land in which to live, how He loved them and protected them always. These stories started to make me wonder about religion. I could not get over the way this God took care of His people. It sounded as though Jehovah was real, more real than any of the gods our people worshipped. He actually communicated with His people through His prophets. He seemed very powerful, like I thought a god should be. I did not want to worship a god that had been made by someone in the market. I did not want to follow gods who asked for human sacrifices, but who were not able to do anything about slaves who insulted and hit them. Fish Man's God sounded very different. He wanted a relationship with His people.

One of God's commandments was to love Him and serve only Him. The gods I grew up hearing about did not ask for love. Actually, we used them to get what we wanted. If we wanted good weather, then we made a sacrifice to one god. If we wanted victory in battle, we made a sacrifice to a different god. There was never any talk about a relationship. That alone intrigued me.

Even though Jonah was not happy about coming to give us God's message because he hated the Assyrians and did not want God to save us, I was interested in his God. Jonah may have been hard-hearted, but his God was merciful. That was not a character quality of any of the gods I knew about. I asked Jonah if his God might be interested in a young girl who liked wonderful stories. He laughed long and hard at this question. Then he looked at me and took my hand.

"God says that we will find Him when we seek Him with all our heart. Seek Him through prayer, and He will be your God."

"Even though I am just a girl, an Assyrian girl at that?"

"Yes, even so."

That was my last private conversation with Jonah. The following evening, I brought him before my parents as he was strong enough, and he was demanding to see them. He explained what had happened and really made me look pretty good in his telling of the story. He made me sound like a very brave girl for rescuing him. My mother, for once, did not sigh when she heard a story about me. After dinner, Jonah started to tell my parents what he had begun telling me. I was listening from behind the curtain, as I was not allowed to stay for conversation with the adults.

Jonah was a strange man. He seemed to have grown somewhat fond of me, but he definitely did not care for us, Assyrians, as a people. He ranted on about how evil we were and how God was going to judge us and destroy our city if we did not change our behavior and seek His forgiveness. I could not believe my parents were listening to this from him. I thought my father would have him thrown out of our house. Instead, my parents listened to all of his insults and yelling, and with tears in their eyes, asked what exactly they should do to prevent this destruction from happening to our city.

If you are familiar with the story, you will know that Jonah preached his message to the entire city, and our leaders called the people to do just what he told them. I was amazed. I wondered if they felt the same way I did about the Hebrew God. If they listened to this God, then why did they also follow all of the other silly idols perched about in the many temples within the city? Jonah had told me that Jehovah demanded that He be worshipped as the one and only God.

Jonah did not stay with us for very long after giving us his message. He may not have wanted his God to spare our city, but he did take a liking to me. He encouraged me to seek his God. He reminded me of all that I had learned from him. If I wanted to be rescued and loved by God, then I needed to follow the teachings I had learned from Jonah about Him.

Jonah's God intrigued me so much. From what I learned through Jonah's stories, his rants, and from what I saw on the shore that first day, I decided that there really was a God named Jehovah, and I would follow Him. His mercy and love drew me to want to know more about Him.

How could I ever have guessed that a young Assyrian girl could come to know the one and only God because of an experience with a river monster and his regurgitated lunch? That day on the banks of the Tigris was a turning point. If I had the time, I would tell you all of the details of war and destruction that came to our city because we did not follow through for long on what Jonah had told us. We quickly forgot about Jehovah and His warning. For my family and I there were losses, rescues, and moves across deserts.

For now, I will simply say that Jehovah has always been with me, providing for me and loving me. It took me years to learn more about Him, but I knew the most important thing from the very beginning. He is a God of love and mercy. He will go to extremes to show His love for people, even sending a river monster to carry His messenger with His message of deliverance. He will always find a way to show His love. And no matter who you are, or where you live, God's message is still the same. He longs to love you and give you the power to love Him in return.

3

Rahab

People see me as unsavory, hopeless, hardened, and lost. Who would associate with me except, of course, for men? I am a tainted woman—a woman who sells herself to men for their pleasure. I was once beautiful beyond words. That beauty has faded considerably now. The beauty that can be sold only lasts so long. However, there is a deeper beauty that I was to learn about, but I am getting ahead of myself.

Let me go back to the beginning, so you will understand my story better.

I grew up in a bustling city with lots of entertainment and activities. All of my friends enjoyed celebrating, so as a young adult, I began drinking quite too much wine. Of course, we had to get the wine from somewhere other than our homes. Our parents would never have allowed us to drink as much as we did. I was very beautiful, popular, and sought after by boys my age. But even more flattering, men my father's age wanted to be with me. They had money to buy me the best wine and expensive gifts. I learned quickly to use my beauty to get what I wanted.

I decided that instead of marrying the dull man my parents had chosen for me, I would pursue a more independent life. I would choose whom I wanted to spend time with and for how long. I would take care of myself and be in control. I did not need a husband to complete me. Men were weak anyway. They could be so easily manipulated by their lusts.

I knew that I was a great disappointment to my parents. They wanted to see me married and settled down like parents do. But there was something in me that drove me to seek after different things: excitement, danger, thrill. All of these things led me down a very depraved path that ended only in loneliness and shame. There was no one at the end of the day that really cared about me. No one was there to take care of me when I was unwell. No one asked how I was feeling or what my dreams were. I was really, hopelessly alone, but I had gotten what I set out to get. I was in charge of my life.

By some standards, I was living quite well, actually. I resided in one of the best areas of the city in a lovely home. You see our city was quite a place. We were considered a stronghold. The walls around our city were doubled. The inner wall was 30 feet high and 6 feet wide. The outer wall was the same height but 12 feet wide. My home was inside the city walls. It was spacious and beautifully appointed. I had the money to indulge in everything necessary to make my visitors comfortable.

Some evenings there were even chariot races on the top of the outer wall that protected our city. Those times were good ones for my business. There was always heavy drinking along with betting on the different drivers. The winners often celebrated their victories with me. One of the drivers, named Josef, was a special client of mine. He was handsome and generous. He was also demanding and occasionally, cruel. Surprisingly, I found myself beginning to care for Josef, perhaps even love him. I began to dream about the future, and in all my dreams, he was beside me. Somehow, he slithered past my defenses and broke through the walls I had built around my heart. I thought those walls were impenetrable like the walls around our city. But Josef's handsome face, strength, and enthusiasm for life enthralled me. I started to convince myself that he cared for me. Was he beginning to want more from our relationship, also?

Unfortunately, I was, once again, lying to myself. This reality violently struck me in the face one night. Josef had come to my home after losing a chariot race. He was angry and had been drinking heavily. He was carelessly cruel with me. I told myself that it was nothing. I made excuses for him as I tried to recover from his brutality. After all, I did not expect gentleness from any man. Weren't they more beast than anything? However, what destroyed me that night was not his physical violence, but his cutting words. He started to yell and curse at me saying I was no more valuable than his worthless horse that could not win a chariot race.

"Perhaps, I need to buy myself a new horse and a new woman. Both of you are worn out and pitiful. I am a winner and need winners around me, not losers. Too bad you cannot shoot women and put them out of their misery like we can with horses." He laughed viciously and stormed out slamming the heavy wooden door behind him.

I was stunned. I felt his words like a slap to the face. How could I have allowed myself to believe, to hope, that I was special to him? I meant no more to him than his horse. Maybe even less. I felt so cold and empty. Something in me turned to stone as I stood there thinking about this man that I dreamed might actually care for me, Rahab the woman, not just Rahab the prostitute. The walls around my heart went up even higher, and in that moment I made a vow. I would never again allow myself to hope or dream. These things were for the weak and the stupid. Reality was stark and cold, and I needed to accept it and move forward. There was no such thing as love. People simply did what was necessary to survive, just like the animals. Even parents raised their children carefully so that in their old age, those children would be there to take care of them. It was just good, solid logic. Love had nothing to do with it. I needed nothing from anyone. I would continue to take care of myself and do whatever was necessary to survive. Josef and men like him were all there were in the world. Never again would I be deceived by a handsome face, smooth words, or virility. As long as they could provide the money for me to live as I wished and save for my old age, I would use them as they used me. When I was finished with them, I would toss them aside as I had been tossed aside.

As I looked out through my window that night, I found the brightest star in the sky, raised my fist, and vowed aloud, "Never again will I be fooled into believing in hopes or dreams. There is no such thing as love. I will care for myself and do whatever it takes to survive this life."

Sometimes I can hardly believe that was me. I was a prostitute and proud of it. I supported myself and lived in style at a time when most women were dependent on men for their basic needs like food and shelter.

But even though I tried not to notice, I knew that something was missing in my life. Believe me, I tried hard to fill myself up. I visited the market place often and was well-known by the local merchants. Even so, no matter what I bought or what I did, I still felt this emptiness. A desire for something unknown was growing in me. I did not understand it. I did not know at the time, but God was calling me—me, Rahab, the harlot.

Shortly after making my vow, the city began to buzz with information about the Israelites. They were camped not far from our city. Not that the leaders were truly afraid of them, because ours was a fortified city. But we had heard stories about the extraordinary things their God had done—the escape from Egypt, the plagues, the drowning of the entire Egyptian army. Terrifying events.

It was quite late one evening as I made my way across the city center toward my home. As I rounded the corner, I noticed two men sitting on the edge of the well wall. They were obviously not men from Jericho. Their mode of dress was different, and they looked tired, travel-weary. They must have come to town some time that day and not been able to find a place to stay. Our city was not known for its hospitality. None of the townsmen had invited these travelers to stay the night with their family. I am sure they were preparing to pass a rather cool and uncomfortable night right there in the town square.

I approached the men slowly and asked if they needed a place to stay. They would pay for the privilege, of course. I figured they were desperate enough to pay for the chance to sleep inside instead of on the hard stones in the square.

The taller of the two men looked directly into my eyes and smiled. He thanked me for the invitation and accepted my kind offer. I wanted to tell him that I was far from kind and would probably charge them more than I should for the privilege of sleeping indoors for the night. Somehow, my lips would not form the words. He waited patiently, looking at me without the hint of anything more than thankfulness. His companion shifted uncomfortably back and forth on his feet. Finally, I cleared my throat and told them to follow me. It was not far to my home from the square.

When we arrived, I offered them the opportunity to share my room. Jacob, the spokesman, looked uncomfortable for a moment. He shared a look with his friend. Then he turned to me and replied, "We could not dishonor you this way. Is your husband not home for the evening?"

From my dress and appearance they must have known that I was not married. I scoffed and swore at him. "Don't play games with me. You and your friend here must know what I am. You will not get out of the fee for the evening by pretending otherwise. I am not young and untried. Don't try to fool me."

Jacob seemed taken aback by my comments. He took a moment to compose himself before responding. "I am sorry to have offended you. My friend and I will leave if you prefer, but we cannot in good conscience share your room. We would greatly appreciate it if we might, perhaps, use your roof for the evening. We will be happy to pay for the place to stay."

What kind of men were these? I had not met men like this in a long time. Had I ever? Jacob and Salmon stood at a respectful distance. Salmon looked at his worn shoes while Jacob looked at my face. Was that tenderness I saw? My heart raced but so did my anger. I wanted to throw these men back out into the cold night. I did not need this.

But instead I found myself answering, "You may use the roof. There is fresh straw there to help you stay warm and dry."

Where did those words come from? Before I could change my mind, Jacob and Salmon were thanking me for this kindness and heading for the steps to the roof.

Over the next couple of days, the men remained in my home. They left early in the morning and returned late at night. They did not seem to do any business, and this caused me to wonder what they were doing in Jericho. One night, I made my way up the steps to the roof. Salmon and Jacob jumped to their feet as they heard me approaching. I asked if I might speak with them for a moment.

"What exactly are you doing in our city? You are busy every day but do not conduct any business. You talk with the men in the square, yet ask no questions about business opportunities. I am curious as to why you are here. I feel as though you are planning something. I want to know the truth. I want a cut of whatever you are involved in. After all, I have given you a safe place to stay and have not mentioned any of my suspicions to the city elders."

Jacob seemed as if he had been expecting my questions. Salmon appeared a bit more unsettled. As usual, Jacob spoke on behalf of the two men. His words were like thunder in my ears. It could not be true.

"We are Israelite spies. God has promised to give us this city as a part of our promised land. We have been sent ahead to survey the city and report back to our leaders. We will not lie to you."

Israelite spies? The Israelites' God was renowned to be mighty above all other gods. Had He not single-handedly crushed the Egyptians and set free the entire slave population? The terrifying stories of rivers turning to blood and frogs infesting the land, along with the deaths of all the first-born in Egypt were enough to give even the soundest sleepers nightmares.

Should I run to the home of the city leader? I knew where he lived. There were several times when I had visited his home secretly late at night while his wife was already asleep. Should I expose this threat to our city? I did not want our city destroyed like Egypt had been destroyed.

Even as these thoughts raced through my mind, I also had so many questions. Why did they come to me? Was this a coincidence? How could I save myself? My family? Could we be victorious over the Jewish God? Then I wondered why they had been so honest with me. Didn't they know I held their lives in my hands?

When I asked them about this, they said, "We serve the God who creates all life. He is the One who holds our lives in His hands. He created us in our mothers' wombs. He will take care of us. We are His beloved children. You are not the one who will decide our fate. God is in control of all things."

I was shocked again. Did they really believe this? Did they really believe that one of the gods would stoop down to love them individually and really care about what happened to them? Even as I thought they were crazy to believe this, my heart and mind were whispering something else.

What if this is true? What if there is such a God out there who does care, who does love people, who does control lives? My heart beat faster; my palms grew sweaty. I could not sit still any longer. I rose and started to pace. The voices in my head were arguing. A part of me screamed not to believe a word they said about their God. I had made a vow to never again dream or hope. Yet what these men were saying was creating a desire in me. A yearning I had not been able to completely squelch began to build inside of me. I raised my face to the sky and yelled in frustration. I could not allow this wall I had carefully constructed around my heart to crack. My heart could not survive another disappointment if what they claimed turned out to be another lie.

Jacob came to stand beside me. He put his hand on my shoulder and with great tenderness said, "Our God brought us to you, to this house. It is not a coincidence that you are the one who has housed us and taken care of us the past two days. He chose you for this job. He loves you also."

At those words, I shrugged off his hand and turned to look at him, disbelief in my eyes. I snarled at him like a wounded dog that has just been kicked again. "Don't try to stop me from revealing your evil plot to the city leaders by trying to flatter me. I know who and what I am. I am not going to fall for your lies and false promises. I learned my lessons long ago."

Salmon slowly rose from his seat in the straw, and came to join Jacob, who was standing by my side. For the first time since I met him, Salmon spoke.

"Rahab, do not be afraid to believe in God's love. He has promised to give us beauty in place of ashes, the oil of joy instead of mourning. He says He will take away our spirit of heaviness and replace it with the garment of praise. Believe us when we say, He is in charge of all events. He will take care of you during this battle. All you have to do is ask. He is faithful and will do what He promises. You have built a wall around your heart because of years of pain and abuse. Allow God to take it down. He will be gentle in removing each stone that you have labored to put in place. He will replace your stone wall with a heart of flesh that will be able to love and be loved in return. He delights in bringing life into places of darkness and hopelessness. I know this is true. He did this for me. Do not be afraid. Allow yourself to be loved. Only believe."

There was such conviction in his voice, such intensity shining in his eyes. He was no longer the man looking down at his shoes. He was a beacon of hope offering water to a thirsty soul.

Love—that was what I was looking for. We talked late into the night. They told me such stories; were they too good to be true? Yet, I found myself beginning to hope as they spoke with great love and reverence about their God.

The next morning, I discovered that somehow the city leaders had discovered the presence of the spies hiding in my house. Guards arrived to question me. My maid informed me that they were at the door waiting. I dressed hastily and descended the narrow stone stairway to greet them.

"Where are the spies, woman?" they spat in disgust.

"They heard you were coming and fled during the night," I lied easily. "They fashioned a rope and let themselves down over the wall as I slept. I discovered their disappearance just this morning."

The guards looked at each other, not sure if to believe me or not. They shoved past me and entered the stairwell. I was so glad to be able to trust my maid. Only she knew that I had hastily hidden Jacob and Salmon under some flax on the rooftop before talking with the soldiers. I was not convinced that the four trained men would not be able to find the spies.

In that moment, I did something I had never done before in my life. I prayed. I bowed my head as the men raced up the stairs.

"God, if You are real, then rescue Jacob and Salmon. They say You love them. Protect them from these men today. If they are found, they will be tortured and killed."

Perhaps it was not the most eloquent prayer ever spoken, but it was heartfelt. I was not sure if this Hebrew God would hear me, but I could not stop myself from hoping.

I took the stairs two at a time, racing to catch up with the guards. Just as I entered the living area, the guards were getting ready to take the stairs up to the roof. In that moment, a disturbance was heard from just outside the window. The ugliest guard who looked like his nose had been broken many times, rushed over to peer outside. He leaned out and gazed down. The noise built.

"You there," he shouted at the top of his lungs, "what is going on out there?" We could only hear a mumble in response. The guard started to curse loudly. He pulled his head back into the room and turned sharply.

"Apparently what the prostitute says is true. The spies have been spotted heading towards the hills. They must have gotten a tip that we were coming." He looked at me with such hatred. I took a step backwards involuntarily and held my breath. Would Jacob and Salmon be saved, while I was beaten to death by these violent men, in my own home?

Sabreel, my maid, stepped forward and spoke in her no nonsense voice. "Are you men going to stand there staring at my mistress and allow these Hebrew dogs to escape?" The question grabbed their attention. They dashed out of the room and pounded down the stairs. The echo of the door slapping open ricocheted up the stairs.

Sabreel slowly made her way over to me. She took my cold, shaking hands between her work-worn palms. What would I do without her? As I looked into her face, I noticed a familiar twinkle in her old, brown eyes. She was up to something. I knew this look.

"What have you done?" I asked, somewhat nervously.

"Look outside the window and see if you recognize the young man below."

After doing what she suggested, I realized that the man who had obviously spoken to the soldier was Sabreel's grandson, Aabid. He had gathered a group of people who now stood below, pointing toward the hills and shouting about spies, enemies, and a chase. Sabreel must have put him up to this. How she accomplished this on such short notice, I did not know. I just knew that Jacob and Salmon needed to flee the city as quickly as possible.

With that thought running through my mind, I raced to the roof, with Sabreel making her way a bit more sedately. After exposing their hiding place, we discussed how to safely get them out of the city without being seen. Going out a window during the night seemed like the best idea. We engaged Aabid in our plot, again. With all of us working together, we were able to help Jacob and Salmon escape. Before they left, they made a promise to me. Because I had helped them to survive, they would spare my life when Israel attacked. I would have to tie a scarlet cord to the window. Everyone who was inside my house would be spared. I knew I could trust these men. In the short time they had been in my house, I had learned so much. I had begun to hope again.

Yes, I hid these men. Yes, I lied to the officials who searched for them. Yes, I risked my life to protect the enemies of our city. They said that their God loved individuals, even a woman like me. He would accept me as His daughter. He would forgive. Oh, how I needed forgiveness. What did I have to lose? Some might say that I could have been killed for what I did. But they do not understand that I was already dead on the inside. I was longing for freedom, for life, for love, for forgiveness, and all of these were offered to me freely. What a mighty God who saves and forgives even a wretch like me.

We were not sure exactly when the attack on the city would happen. We just knew that we had to be ready when it did begin. As it was, we had some warning. It was not too long before the Israelite army entered the area surrounding our city. The people were terrified. The city leaders were terrified. Because of the stories of the Hebrew God, they knew that not even high, wide walls could keep the army from being victorious.

As we waited for the attack to begin, a heaviness settled over the city. One morning I awoke to the noise of thousands of heavily armored soldiers moving. It sounded like thunder. There were also trumpet blasts. Each blast of a trumpet seemed to proclaim victory. The soldiers on the streets of Jericho were tense. The soldiers stationed on the high walls watched and waited.

Strangely enough, on the first day after their arrival, the mighty Israeli army just marched around the entire city, blowing trumpets. The soldiers themselves were completely silent. It was eerie and unsettling. The tension built throughout that first day. When would they actually attack us? This strategy continued for the next five days. Six days they marched in silence around the city with only the noise of trumpets and the footfalls of thousands of soldiers.

Inside my home, we were quiet but unsettled. I had tied the scarlet cord to my window as Jacob and Salmon commanded. My family was with me in the house along with Sabreel, Aabid and his family. We were hopeful that the two men would keep their promise to us, and we would be spared in the attack. But there were doubts about how they could accomplish this. How could Jacob have told all these thousands of soldiers that of all the citizens' homes in the city, mine was the one home that should spared? It was hard to understand and so hard to believe.

Aabid had brought his sword with him when he arrived with his family. But how could he fight a trained army? I knew nothing of weapons except for the small dagger that was beneath my pillow. Sabreel was too old to fight anyone. She could give someone a good talking to for sure, but she would be useless in a physical fight. We had no choice but to trust the spies.

On the morning of the seventh day, I awoke feeling different than I had all week. I felt as if something momentous was about to happen. I arose and went straight to the window as I had each morning. Looking out, I noticed that the army was once again assembling and getting ready to begin its march around the city. I was a bit disappointed. How long would this continue? As I dressed for the day, I could hear the thump of thousands of feet, marching, marching. The trumpets were sounding.

The noise had become so familiar to our household. We just went about our business as usual, or as normally as one can when forced to hide inside a house for days on end.

As the morning wore on, I realized that the marching had not stopped at the usual time. This made me wonder what was going on. I hurried to the window to look beyond the wall. The back of the army was going by the window for the second time that day. This was unusual. Why were they marching a second time?

Throughout the day, the army continued to march and blow their trumpets. Inside the house we kept count. It was difficult to focus on anything else all day. Late in the afternoon, I stood at the window watching the action. I could not believe that the soldiers would continue marching. They had circled Jericho six times today. I wished I knew why. I wished I knew what was happening. As the front of the army came into view, I anxiously watched to see if they would stop the tedious marching. The dust created by thousands of feet, filled the air. The marching did not falter or stop. The army moved steadily past my window, silent but for the incessant, thundering footsteps. I whirled away frustrated. This waiting was driving me mad. I could only imagine what the soldiers of Jericho were feeling. Had they been able to sleep during the past week?

As the sun began to set, we decided to sit for our evening meal. It had been a long and tiring day at the end of a long and frustrating week. Even Sabreel who was usually so patient, had been testy with her daughter-in-law. Just as we were to begin our meager meal, there was a burst of trumpet blasts. It was a different sound from what we had experienced all week. The blasts were louder, longer, and more dynamic. Along with the melodies of the trumpeters, shouting began. It seemed to build and build until it was so loud that I covered my ears with my hands. Even that did not drown out the din.

Through the window we could see the army standing in the floating dust, beating their swords and spears against their shields, yelling at the tops of their lungs. The musicians were blowing with all their might. It was a majestic challenge even though they still made no move to attack the city. We looked at each other wondering what this new tactic meant.

It was just a few moments later that a new, louder noise could be heard over the din of the army. It sounded like the most intense thunderstorm ever. The rumbling shook my bones. I felt the floor tremble beneath my feet. I looked into Sabreel's face. We had been together since I had moved out of my parents' home. She looked as terrified as I felt. Were we about to lose our lives? None of us knew just what was going on. We could hear the yells and screams of the soldiers on the top of the wall. It was complete chaos. We all huddled together weeping and trembling in the center of the room. We heard what sounded like monstrous thuds all around us as the entire wall shook and vibrated. I closed my eyes as tightly as I could, somehow hoping that would block out the sounds around me. Dust streamed into the room through the window. For the second time in my life, I prayed. It was more like hysterical babbling, I admit, but it was all I was capable of at the time.

"Save us, God. Save us."

I think I must have blacked out after that. The next thing I remember was Aabid's face peering down at me. I noticed that it was coated with the sandy dust of the flat lands surrounding the city. Even his black eyelashes were white with dust. There were streaks down his cheeks. I thought that he must have been crying which was certainly odd. Aabid was tough. Why would he be crying? Before I could find an answer in my fuzzy brain, another thought registered. Light was streaming into my house. I looked over toward the window. The window had been transformed into an opening the size of a doorway. It looked as though the wall had crumbled.

My mind cleared at the sight. I sat up quickly, and the room started to spin. Closing my eyes, I gulped in some air. It was still filled with dust. My deep breath caused me to cough, and my eyes watered. This explained the tear tracks on Aabid's cheeks. When I opened my eyes, I noticed that all of us were still alive. However, instead of being safely in my comfortable home, we were sitting on the floor of a shell of my former house. I turned back to Aabid.

"What happened?" I asked. My voice sounded weak and strained to my ears.

"The walls around the city as far as I can see have fallen down. Not one stone seems to be left piled on another. We are the only section that I can see which is still standing." His voice was filled with fear and awe.

None of us knew what to do next. Should we leave the house? Were the stairs intact to allow us to exit? Could we climb out of what was once the window? I could feel hysteria building. I tried to calm myself by slowing my breathing. So far, Jacob's promise to me was proving to be true. I would hold onto that and trust that we would not be crushed as this section of the wall crumbled beneath our feet.

I slowly rose to my feet. I struggled to come up with an idea about what we should do next. Jacob had not given me any directions other than to tie the cord to the window. I had followed that direction. Now what?

As I thought about my next move, I heard the sound of rocks falling on the inside section of the wall. Then we heard shouting. It sounded like directions were being yelled. Before we could react, a familiar head appeared in the opening in the inner wall. I recognized the face immediately even though it was partially covered by a helmet and streaked with dust and grime. The smile was the same as the one I had witnessed many times while this remarkable man stayed in my home.

"Jacob," I shouted with great joy. Sabreel rushed forward shouting and laughing. She reached out her arms and wrapped them around him almost lifting him off the ground in her excitement. Right behind him, Salmon appeared looking just as grimy as Jacob. We were all so relieved that we started laughing and clapping. I was especially happy to see Salmon.

I could continue to tell you what happened in my life, but that would take so long. Let me just summarize by saying that God was certainly gracious to me. He kept His promises to forgive, love unconditionally, and give me hope and a future. His grace to me was amazing. And not only did He forgive me, but He gave me honor and dignity that I did not deserve. He has called me a hero of the faith....me. And if that were not enough, He allowed me to marry. You may have guessed my husband's name, Salmon. Who would have thought that a man of such integrity would be interested in a former prostitute? Certainly God has been gracious to me.

We had a son, Boaz; maybe you have heard of him. He was the grandfather of Jesse, who was the father of David, King David from whose bloodline came Jesus, our Savior.

God broke down the carefully built wall around my heart. He brought freedom to this captive. He gave me a future I could never have imagined. He showed His favor to me. He comforted me. He bestowed on me a crown of beauty and gladness. He called me *righteous* and *a woman who displays His splendor.*

What a mighty, gracious God I serve.

4

Ravi's Sister

avi is not a name you will recognize from your Bible. He is not mentioned by his given name, but you have probably heard his story. There were many times that both he and I were part of the crowd that followed Jesus as He walked through our small town and along some of the lonely roads just outside of town. We tried to understand the words He spoke, but so many times, we just felt confused.

Jesus was a man like any other in our village. He dressed similarly and spoke our language. However, I did notice that His sandals were very worn. The seams of his garments were frayed. Didn't He have the money to replace them? Everywhere He went, a large crowd followed. Sometimes they were loud and created chaos in our small village. Many of my parents' friends were upset by the noise and disturbance His followers caused. You might have been irritated too, if you lived in our area.

Sometimes, Jesus' words were awfully confusing, and sometimes they were terrifying. Always, they were difficult to interpret. He often used stories to illustrate His point, but these stories left me feeling even more bewildered. Once I heard Him teach about trusting God. This was not an unusual teaching except that He spoke of trusting God, not only in our desperate times, but especially when things were going well in our lives. He said we tended to forget about God when life was flowing smoothly because we relied on our own resources. This really challenged Ravi, my brother, and me. Our parents always taught us to work hard, use our talents, and rely on our own efforts. Both of us took pride in our diligence. Ravi had become quite wealthy because of his hard work.

The other teaching of Jesus that caused me many sleepless nights was His teaching about heaven. He promised that He was going to heaven to prepare a place for us so that we could be with Him and the Father. No rabbi in the synagogue had ever claimed anything like this.

That week, when Jesus visited our village, was an unsettling one. I found myself hurrying through my chores with Mama just so I could run out and find the crowds that surrounded Jesus and try to get a glimpse of Him. Occasionally, I was able to get so close to Jesus that I could see into His eyes as He spoke and notice even the smallest change of expression on His face. So close that I could see the frayed edges of His clothing and smell the smoke on His skin from His dinner bonfire the night before.

His words were curious. He spoke of things that the rabbis in the synagogue never discussed. He never talked of rules and doing what was right. He talked more about love, loving God and loving each other. And yet, when He spoke, there was an authority to His words that not even the most important of the rabbis had ever captured.

The most shocking thing I heard Him say all week was that we were to love even our enemies. I was so upset by His words. Obviously, He did not have enemies. He did not know what it felt like to have someone betray a trust. I immediately started to remember my former best friend, Salome, who had wounded me deeply just about three months ago. I was surprised to feel the pain of my nails digging into my palms. I unclenched my hands and tried to focus once again on what the Teacher was saying. He was still talking about forgiveness. I no longer wanted to listen. I could tell some others in the crowd did not like what He was saying either. A group of men to my right were muttering together. I recognized one of my father's friends, Ezra, just before he looked over my way. I ducked behind a rather large lady on my left and scurried home, thankful not to have been caught. My father would have been very angry with me.

But I was so unsettled by Jesus' teaching about forgiveness. I longed to talk with my parents about this, but my father was already upset about Jesus being in the village. He felt as though the mob that traveled with Him would cause trouble for our people. He refused to allow us to talk about Jesus at our evening meal. For most of the week, my family ate in uncomfortable silence. Our dinners were usually filled with animated discussions, laughter, and good-natured arguments between my father and brother. Mama would simply shake her head and sigh when those two started arguing about business or politics. When I reflect back on that time, I am sure that both Mama and Papa must have guessed that I had been sneaking off to see Jesus. Maybe Ezra had seen me after all and told my parents. As my brother always said, I never could keep a secret. If my mouth did not blurt out the truth, it was usually clear in my expressions. Even though they must have known I was up to something, they never asked me where I was spending those hours, and I did not want to tell them. Better to apologize than to ask permission, as my brother always said.

I was a good Jewish girl, most of the time. I tried my best to do what I was told. I tried to obey my parents' teaching and follow all of the rules the best I could. However, I knew in my heart that something was missing. Late one night, after dinner I talked with my brother. He was so smart and had made a good deal of money over the past couple of years. He was the success story of our family. We were known to be wealthy, but my brother had surpassed my own father's wealth in just a few short years of business. Many people in our village were in awe of my brother's accomplishments. Whatever he touched flourished and made money overnight. However, even with all of this success, my brother remained a faithful Jew and a loyal son. He did what was required of him and tried to live as our forefathers had ordained. But he seemed to understand my emptiness as I spoke to him about it that night.

"Ravi, something is missing in my life."

"Yes, Myrna, a husband." He never stopped teasing me about the fact that I still was not engaged to a nice young man from the village.

"No silly, don't tease me. This is something serious. I have tried to follow Papa's teaching on our Jewish laws, as you also have done. But do you not feel unsettled by the words of Jesus? He speaks, and it is like a fresh breeze blowing in before a storm. His words bring comfort but with a swirling of emotion at the same time. They confuse me yet make me want something more. I don't know how to put these feelings into words."

Although my brother listened to me that night, he did not have any answers for me. He had also been following the Rabbi as He traveled through our village. He understood what I was saying, and I could tell he felt the same tension as he thought about what Jesus proclaimed about the Kingdom of God. One of the things that confused us was that Jesus kept talking about our attitudes and motivations and not about what rules we followed. Both Ravi and I longed to sit down with Jesus and ask Him exactly what we needed to do to be worthy of heaven. As we ended our conversation that night, I knew that both of us were frustrated.

The next day, Jesus was to leave our village and journey on to the next town. I knew that I had to see Him one last time before He left. Perhaps, this time I would understand His words and find the truth that would quench this thirst taking over my life.

The following morning, my brother and I slipped out of the house early, before our parents were stirring. We ran through the narrow streets toward the place we knew Jesus would be. As we came around a corner, there was His band of followers. They had already started off on their journey. Had we missed the Rabbi?

My brother looked back at me and darted off down a side lane. I tried to work my way through the group of men and women who were all moving out of the village. Just as I was making my way to the front of the pack, everyone abruptly stopped walking. I bumped into the woman in front of me in my haste and apologized quickly, my head down. I was not sure I wanted to be recognized in the crowd and have to explain to my parents what I was doing in this group of ruffians, as Papa called them.

As I continued to struggle toward the front of the group, I heard a familiar voice. It was Ravi. I hurriedly turned toward his voice. I edged my body between a woman and an older man at her side. The top of my head brushed his long grey beard as I bent down to squeeze between them.

What was Ravi saying to the Rabbi? I peered over the head of an old woman who was bent forward at the waist leaning on a crooked stick. The Rabbi stood just to her right and a step ahead. His hand was resting on her shoulder, and she seemed to be leaning into His touch. I recognized some of His disciples standing close to Him. The fisherman, Peter, was just off to my right. He was rather scary looking, fierce and rugged. His eyes scanned the crowd looking for anyone who might want to harm the Rabbi.

As I looked past Peter, I saw Ravi kneeling in front of the Rabbi, in the dust of the path. He was blocking the whole group from leaving the village. I could feel the restlessness of the people behind me. I glanced at Peter. He looked irritated and angry, too. He peered at Jesus as if to seek permission to remove this intruder from the path, so they could be on their way. Jesus shook His head ever so slightly and then looked at Ravi kneeling in front of Him.

"Good teacher, what must I do to inherit eternal life?" Ravi's voice was clear and direct.

I was embarrassed to see my wealthy, respected brother kneeling in the dirt and asking such a question in front of all these people. Haven't we learned the answer to this question in synagogue since we were young children?

But a part of me knew that this was the most important question ever asked, for my brother and me. What would Jesus say?

His response was not really an answer. Actually, He asked a seemingly unrelated question instead of answering Ravi.

"Why do you call Me good? No one is good, except God alone." He said this with a curious look on His face as though He was being playful. I held my breath without even realizing it.

Ravi seemed confused and did not reply. The crowd remained silent. It appeared to me that the whole universe was waiting for the next words of Jesus.

After a long pause, Jesus continued. "Do not murder. Do not commit adultery. Do not steal. Do not give false testimony, and do not defraud. Honor your father and mother."

What a disappointment. These were the same teachings we heard in synagogue each week. We had tried all of our lives to live out these teachings.

Jesus moved past my brother to continue His planned journey out of the village. People were ready to forget about the interruption and move on to the next adventure. Abruptly, my brother scrambled ahead of the group and positioned himself directly in front of Jesus' path again.

My brother was the best son, brother, and Jew. He tried to keep these commandments. From our conversation last night, I know that my brother is feeling what I am feeling since hearing Jesus speak: a longing we cannot identify. This eternal life that Jesus speaks about is confusing for us. There is something we cannot define, but something we know we were created to experience.

"Teacher, all these things I have kept since I was a boy."

Some people in the crowd laughed uncomfortably; others grumbled at my brother's response. But they did not know him, and they did not know that tone of voice. They did not hear the desperation in his words. I heard the grief, the yearning, the question beneath the words.

I have tried all of this before, Teacher, and it has not worked. It has not brought me satisfaction. Don't leave me with just this. I cannot live without this life you speak of any longer. Do not walk away and leave me with just this. Isn't there more than this? There must be more than this.

I waited. I looked at Jesus' face. He had the same expression again—a slight smile, with genuine compassion and pure love shining in His eyes. He focused on Ravi as though he was the only person in the world. Ravi continued to stare at Jesus, waiting for an answer. When He spoke to Ravi, His answer was, again, unexpected.

"One thing you lack. Go, sell everything you have, and give to the poor, and you will have treasure in heaven. Then, come and follow Me."

What did He say? I glanced at Ravi's face. There was shock, then deep confusion. Ravi raised his eyes to Jesus' face. Sadness flooded his features. He rose slowly as if his body was weighted down with the load a camel should carry. His shoulders, usually so broad and erect, sagged like my grandfather's.

Did Jesus know what He was asking? My brother was one of the richest men in town. Again the crowd was whispering, laughing, and talking about what had happened. As Ravi reluctantly stepped aside, he glanced back at Jesus. I could almost hear his thoughts.

You ask too much of me. You do not realize what You are asking. This is the one thing I cannot do. This is the thing that has brought me respect in my family, in my village. You want me to give this all up to follow You? How will I survive without my money, my status, without respect?

Jesus continued to gaze at Ravi. He did not look away until Ravi turned and hurried down the lane.

I was torn. A part of me wanted to run after Ravi to comfort him. But something told me to wait.

Be still and wait.

Just then, Jesus turned and focused on my face directly. He began to speak to His disciples, but He continued to look at me. I could not move. I could not take my eyes off His face.

"How hard it is for the rich to enter the kingdom of God."

The disciples were amazed at these words. The crowd once again became quiet and listened to Jesus. Some seemed upset by His words; some seemed to agree.

Jesus continued. "Children, how hard it is to enter the kingdom of God. It is easier for a camel to go through the eye of a needle than for a rich man to enter the kingdom of God."

My heart ached. Was He really saying that there was no hope for Ravi? For me? This life He had been teaching about, this joy and peace was beyond our reach?

Peter spoke for the group when he asked Jesus with some impatience, "Then who can be saved, Master?" Jesus turned toward Peter, glanced at the crowd, and then fixed His gaze back on me. Slowly, a wonderful smile broke across His face. He tipped back His head and laughed. It was a joyful laugh that brought a lightness into my chest. My toes started tingling, and a warmth flowed from my head and filled me. The Rabbi pierced me with His wonderfully clear gaze again, the smile still on His lips. Quietly, He answered Peter's question, my question.

"With man this is impossible, but not with God." Then He shouted joyously, "With God, all things are possible." He threw His arms up into the air and shouted again laughing, "With My Father all things are possible."

That day changed my life. It transformed my brother's life.

That day, the Rabbi, the lover of us all, planted a seed in Ravi's heart. It was a seed of discontent with his money, a seed of hope that there indeed was more to this life than following rules, a seed that grew over the next few months until Ravi was ready to do what the Good Teacher had instructed him do.

He could not stop thinking about what Jesus had said to him. He had long discussions with my father about the business and about Jesus' words. My father was shocked that Ravi would consider leaving his business and giving up his future as a leader in our village. But slowly over the weeks and months, Ravi came to a decision. He even convinced my father that this was a good idea. I think my father could no longer argue with Ravi's logic and with the changes he saw in my brother's life. Ravi gave it all up. He found ways to give away his wealth to help some of the widows and orphans in our city. He used his money to build homes and feed the needy. He gave and gave until I wondered just how much money my brother actually had.

Truly, all things are possible with God. Ravi's life was transformed. It seemed the more he gave away, the more peace filled his life. As much effort as he once put into making money and earning the respect of his elders, he now poured into helping the people in our city who could do nothing for him and whose opinion of him did not earn him any standing with the city council.

Without leaving our village, he became a disciple of Jesus. He may not have left to physically follow the Rabbi, but he followed His teaching. His actions reminded me of what I had heard Jesus teach about once long ago.

Let your cry come to me, and I will give you an answer, and let you see great and wonderful things, secret things of which you had no knowledge.

I had no idea what Jesus was talking about at the time. But now I am seeing this teaching come to life in my brother's life and also in my own. Jesus knew the cry of our hearts that day in our village when my brother knelt before Him in the dust and pleaded with Him to know about the life that He offered. He read the cry in my eyes across an entire mass of people as He looked at me and proclaimed that all things are possible with God. He has revealed secret things to us about His love and how to really live in this world. He has shown us the secret of joy, peace, contentment, and faith.

Years later, when Peter returned to our village preaching and teaching the Good News, Ravi and I were there along with our entire family, listening and drinking in his words. Our lives were transformed, maybe not overnight, but over time.

The truth is that Jesus is the Good Teacher. He is God, and if you are willing to leave all you hold onto for security in life, and follow Him, then all things will be possible.

He will love you.

He will laugh over you.

He will show you great and wonderful things that you could never have imagined.

5

Martha

My sister has always been my best friend. We shared a room growing up and would often whisper late into the night, sharing our secrets. I remember the time when Mary told me all about how she hid behind a bush making squawking bird noises and convinced old lady Salome that she was about to be attacked. Apparently, she lumbered off toward her house as quickly as possible for such an old lady, muttering all the way, with her skirts hoisted up, showing her red, bony witch's ankles. We laughed over that story many nights. We never did like old lady Salome because she always looked like she had eaten too much salt. Her pale, narrow lips were permanently scrunched into a pucker, and she especially disliked children. She thought we were not much better than the wild dogs that ran through the streets in our village.

Mary and I were as close as two sisters could be. Even though our parents loved us both very much, they were irritated with us many times for keeping them awake with our whispering and giggling. Now that I am older, I realize they were especially concerned that we would awaken our brother, who was often ill.

Our parents entertained friends in our home, and they were always the ones to host gatherings in the neighborhood. I enjoyed helping my mother to prepare for such events. I loved to serve others; it gave me a sense of purpose and fulfillment. My mother regularly told me she thought God had blessed me with the gifts of hospitality and service. Her words made me feel very special and grown up. The truth is that I always enjoyed being active. I liked to be busy and useful. I think it helped me to feel significant. I liked the recognition I received from my parents and their friends. But perhaps I enjoyed the attention too much.

God most definitely blessed me with a wonderful childhood. But in spite of these blessings, I also had to deal with tragedy. My parents died while they were on a trip to visit my mother's friend in another village. My siblings and I were devastated to receive the news. Even though we did not have to worry about money, we felt deep sorrow. There were times we wondered if we would ever laugh again.

However, a few years after our parents' untimely deaths, an amazing thing happened; we met Jesus. We heard He was going to be in the area, and we could hardly believe it because from our youngest memories, we were taught about the promised Messiah. It may sound strange to say it, but we had loved Jesus since we were very young children when our parents had told us all about the Messiah that would one day come to rescue us from our sin. And now He was here. We arose early that morning, and after a hasty breakfast and taking care of the animals, we made our way to the synagogue. We were able to be within a few yards of where Jesus was standing.

He spoke about a passage from Isaiah.

"Yet the LORD longs to be gracious to you; therefore He will rise up to show you compassion. For the LORD is a God of justice. Blessed are all who wait for Him."

His teaching was unlike that of the other rabbis in our synagogue. It is difficult to explain, but Jesus seemed to be speaking about Himself when He quoted the Holy Writings. He had an authority that the other rabbis lacked. When He spoke, I could not take my eyes from Him. My mind did not wander as it often did at other times. I did not think about the chores that needed to be done at the house. His words filled my thoughts.

Blessed are all who wait for Him.

Now, there was an idea that intrigued me. What exactly did Jesus mean by the phrase, *..wait for Him?* I had never understood the concept of waiting. I was more action-oriented. But those three words kept running through my mind. I had no idea how important those three, short words would be to me in the future.

After teaching for about an hour that first day, and answering many questions from the priests and Pharisees who were there, Jesus walked over to us. He asked if He might come to our house for the evening meal. We were startled because we did not expect such a thing to happen. Why had He chosen to approach us? There were many more important people in the crowd. Some of them were horrified that Jesus would ignore them and choose to come to the house of three, rather normal people, instead. But how could we say no to the Messiah of Israel?

I was so nervous about having Jesus in our home. It did not take long, however, for my siblings and me to relax. I have to confess that I was more leary of some of His disciples than I was of Jesus. Peter was so big and quite clumsy. His voice alone could frighten children. His large shoulders filled our house, and I found myself wondering how many things would be knocked over or broken by this giant of a man. Then, there was Judas, who asked so many personal questions about our parents' fortune. He made me feel quite unsettled until Andrew came to the rescue with his comforting words. "Please forgive Judas. He is our treasurer, and so he is always thinking about money. Without him to take care of us, we would forget the need for money for our basic necessities. Sometimes, however, he can be quite intense."

Andrew was calming and kind. I found myself thinking that he would make a wonderful husband for Mary. I guess I was always trying to plan and organize my siblings' lives. Ever since the death of our parents, I have felt responsible for both of them.

By the end of that first evening, we had forged a close friendship with Jesus. He would often come to the house for a meal, a visit, or simply for a rest in the midst of one of His journeys. There was not a time when He came that we didn't learn just by sitting at His feet and listening to His words. He was so filled with love; even in the midst of many demands, He always took the time to make each of us feel cherished and appreciated. Jesus never appeared to be in a hurry. He lived life one moment at a time while still being very clear about what He wanted to accomplish.

Then, one day our brother Lazarus became ill. He had always been more fragile than most of the boys in our village. Sometimes, he was teased by some of the bigger boys for not keeping up during their games. This sickness, however, was more serious than previous times. Optimistically, I thought that with some care, he would get better. But his health worsened. His skin became gray and paper-thin. He grew unresponsive and too weak to lift his head even to sip the soup I prepared for him. Mary and I did not know what we should do.

In desperation we sent word to Jesus. "Please, Lord, come quickly. Lazarus is sick, maybe even dying. Hurry."

Mary and I prayed and wept and hoped every day that Jesus would arrive. Each morning we waited to see Jesus appear at our door. And each night we went to bed hoping that the next day we would hear His voice reassuring us that our brother would be fine. But our hope was in vain. Before Jesus arrived, our beloved Lazarus gasped his last breath. Our grief was overwhelming. How could this have happened? Lazarus was too young to die. How could Jesus have allowed this to happen? Didn't He always say that He would never leave us or forsake us? He would be with us always? When we had needed Him the most, He was nowhere to be found. It was too much. Yes, we knew that Lazarus was now with God, but we felt so alone and abandoned. We had placed our hope in Jesus, but where was He? What was taking Him so long? Did He not care about us after all?

Four long days after Lazarus was placed in the tomb, Jesus entered the village. What a day it was. I shall never forget. I ran out to meet Him when I received word that He was approaching. I was heartbroken, filled with grief over our loss, but also disappointed beyond description. My hopes had been shattered, and I was heartsick. I was ready to throw my questions into Jesus' face. I wanted to grab Him and yell my grief and sorrow and anguish. Instead, as I reached Him, I fell to my knees and cried, "Lord if You had been here my brother would not have died." Sobs violently wracked my body.

Jesus reached down and lifted me to my feet. He wrapped His arms around me and wept with me. Slowly, my weeping ended. Even though there were tears in Jesus' eyes, I noticed a determined look on His face. A feeling of hope re-awakened inside of me. I had come to know this look. I had seen it many times before as Jesus had set out to accomplish some task. As I looked at Him, He spoke.

"I am the resurrection and the life. He who believes in Me will live even though he dies, and whoever lives and believes in Me will never die. Do you believe this?" He asked.

..will never die. What did He mean by that? Lazarus had died. But even as this question ran through my mind, I began to feel an excitement building. I found myself responding, "Yes Lord, I believe that You are the Christ, the Son of God."

The joy in my soul was overwhelming. If only I could really explain the hope that I began to feel at His words. It was almost painful, but so entirely different than the pain of grief that only moments ago had enveloped me. All else was forgotten in that moment, even my grief. Jesus looked toward the tomb with purpose in His eyes, and we hurried in that direction. Mary joined us, along with the crowd who had been at the house mourning with us. Jesus welcomed her with one of His comforting hugs, and we continued on, hand-in-hand, toward the tomb.

Upon arriving at Lazarus's tomb, Jesus asked several of the disciples to roll the huge boulder away from the mouth of the cave. I reached out to touch Jesus' sleeve.

"Lord," I mumbled, "Lazarus has been dead for four days. By now there will be a bad odor." Jesus said nothing; He just looked at me carefully and then at Mary. He briefly closed His eyes and a smile formed on His lips.

Without raising His head or opening His eyes, He said, "Did I not tell you that if you believed you would see the glory of God?" Then He did look at Mary and me with that piercing gaze I had come to expect. He nodded to Peter, and the disciples rushed over to the stone. Peter, by far the strongest of the twelve, counted to three, and they heaved with all their might. Slowly, the immense stone began to roll away from the dark entrance.

I found myself shaking, and I grasped my hands together tightly. I looked over at Mary. She was staring at the tomb's dark doorway. Tears streamed down her face. I could feel goose bumps on my skin. Could this really be happening?

Jesus raised His eyes toward the sky and said, "Father, I thank You that You have heard Me. I know that You always hear Me, but I say this for the benefit of the people standing here, that they may believe that You sent Me." Then, Jesus called Lazarus from his tomb as if He was calling him to come into the house and wash his hands for dinner, as he had done so many times before.

"Lazarus," Jesus commanded, "Lazarus, come out." He called again with delight and authority. "Lazarus."

The crowd quieted. There was a moment of silence as we all held our breath, watching and listening. After a few moments, the crowd began to mutter and grumble. Suddenly, we heard a stumbling and a muffled yell. As Mary and I peered into the gloom of the tomb, out staggered our brother. He was wrapped like a mummy and hopping because the strips of cloth we used to encase him just a few days ago, continued to bind him. The crowd exploded into a cacophony of sound: gasps, screams, cheers, shouts, questions.

For a moment, we were frozen. We simply stared at our brother without moving to help him. Now, it makes me laugh to think of how he looked. At first, I think we were terrified. How could this really be happening? But, Lazarus's muffled voice called our names. At that point, there were tears, but of laughter, celebration, and joy. Jesus' joyous laughter could be heard over and above everyone. We hugged Lazarus so hard and unwrapped the grave clothes as quickly as we could. I could not stop touching him and laughing and weeping all at the same time.

Poor Lazarus looked as bewildered as we felt. He wasn't sure what had happened to him. People were asking him one question after another.

None of us waited to hear his answers before we asked another question. Our minds were having a hard time comprehending the fact that a man who had been dead for four days, had just hopped out of his grave.

Lazarus never liked being the focus of attention, and now an entire crowd was pressing closer than was comfortable. Of course, it was understandable that we had so many questions to ask. They were racing through my mind. I wanted to quiz Jesus and also interrogate Lazarus. But this was not the moment for questions. We needed to get Lazarus home and give him something to eat and drink. He was alive, but he was weak and overwhelmed by the attention.

As the details of what happened were relayed through the crowd toward the back of the gathering, the people surged forward to get a better look. What an amazing miracle we had just witnessed.

Everyone was rejoicing and retelling what they had seen and heard as we made our way back to our house. I could not help but remember the words Jesus had taught that first day in the synagogue.

Blessed are all who wait for Him.

Truly, we were blessed that day. Jesus did this miracle in His time and not ours. Assuredly, the blessing was greater than anything we could have imagined. That day many Jews believed in Jesus, believed that He was the promised Messiah. But, unfortunately, some of our leaders were jealous, envious, and angry. They were fearful of His power. Even the dead could hear His voice and respond when He commanded them to rise again. This was something they had never seen before. This one act of Jesus sealed in the leaders' minds the decision that something must be done to stop Him. Jesus was able to do such astonishing things, now even raising someone from the dead. Surely the crowds would continue to follow Him and leave them behind. They could not allow that to happen.

Although I could talk about that day over and over again, I must share another part of my story. Even after all the time I spent with Jesus and after the amazing miracles I saw Him perform, I still had so much to learn. There was an ugliness hidden deep inside of me.

It revealed itself one day as Jesus and His disciples were passing through town. They stopped at the house for rest and a meal. As usual,

I was bustling around trying to get everything ready for Jesus. For some reason that day, I wanted it all to be perfect. I was struggling with irritation. Something was eating at me. Perhaps I just wanted to be able to tell Mary what she should do, and she was ignoring me. Being the oldest in the family, I confess I often thought it was my duty to be in control of things and point out to my siblings what their responsibilities were and when and how they should be handled. On this day, Mary had clearly told me that she wanted to spend time with the Master. We argued about making a simple meal that would not require so much preparation. I did not agree with her. I kept trying to ignore the feelings of jealousy toward Mary, hoping they would go away. I was so angry that I was the one doing all the work. I made a bit more noise than usual working in the kitchen, hoping that Mary would get the hint and come to help, but she did not. Then I started to get irritated with Jesus. Couldn't He see how I was feeling, how hard I was working? No one noticed me at all. They were all gathered around Jesus, hanging on His every word. Well, I was really steaming. And I was having a very self-righteous pity party. I confess that the thoughts that were going through my head were not exactly holy.

Finally, I could not contain my frustration any longer. I walked right up to Jesus and almost yelled, "LORD don't You care that my sister has left me to do the work all by myself? She is just taking it easy, sitting there and listening, enjoying Your company. Tell her to help me."

Mary gasped aloud at my rudeness. She lowered her eyes, and I could tell that she was embarrassed for me. The disciples were silenced. I am sure they could not believe I had the audacity to raise my voice, question the Lord, and tell Him what He should do. I think Peter was ready to set me sailing on the Sea of Galilee in a leaking boat. I could feel his anger rolling toward me, but as he took a step toward me and opened his mouth to speak, Jesus laid a hand on his arm and stopped him. Peter froze with his mouth open.

If you know anything about Peter, then you know that he often opened his mouth to speak before thinking about what he was going to say, so he was often caught in this pose. It is quite funny now, but back then the humor of the situation was lost on me. We all were frozen in shock, as if we were characters in a painting. I could not believe what I had just done, but I was so worked up that I was not going to back down in front of all those people. I assured myself that Jesus needed to do just what I told Him to do. He needed to tell Mary to get up and come to help me. He needed to recognize how hard I was working and honor me for it. I was right.

Jesus knew what was going on in my thoughts and my heart. He knew my great love for both Him and my sister, Mary. But, He also knew of the pride and desire for control that were growing in me like a cancer. I had come to care so very much about what others thought of me. My entire family had become quite famous after Lazarus was released from his tomb. People had come by the house almost constantly to see him and hear the story. My reputation as a hostess had grown and so had my pride. Caring about my reputation had begun to overshadow my care about the one most important thing in life.

I was also very concerned about the fact that the Pharisees were angry and suspicious of our family. To them, Lazarus was the one who had caused the ruckus that was leading people to believe in Jesus. I was afraid of what could happen to our small family. Fear and pride together were a bad combination. My need to be in control so that life would go smoothly was growing.

Don't You care? What a loaded question to ask Jesus. It seems so silly now, but I know that many of you have probably felt that way at times. Your heart cries out, "Don't You care that I'm the one carrying this burden, Lord? You just don't love me like You love others. They don't seem to have the same trials and difficulties in their lives. I am always called upon to struggle and work so hard. I never seem to get the attention I want."

Jesus did not raise His voice with me or reprimand me. He simply loved me in that moment.

"Martha, Martha." He spoke my name with such love, such comfort. Then He described my feelings so perfectly. "You are worried and upset about many things, but only one thing is needed."

He knew. He knew all of the burdens and anxieties and troubles. I had allowed so much negativity to creep into my heart. I was trying to handle and solve all of my problems on my own. I had allowed many things to distract me from the one thing that was needed: to love my Lord with all of my heart, soul, mind, and strength. I needed to take the time to listen to Him so that I would remember this. When I listened, I was able to hear His words.

You are loved. I will take care of you. You are not alone.

Instead, I had allowed myself to become distracted. I had allowed self-pity born out of my need for recognition and control to creep in and take up residency in my heart. I had forgotten Jesus' words even though He was sitting right here in my house.

Cast all your cares on Me because I care for you. Throw them My way. I will look after you.

Those words had meant so much to me. But somehow, I had allowed worry to wipe away the truth I had learned. Jesus knew I had to be reminded. He always could look at me and know what was in my heart. I can hide my feelings from others and even myself, but not from Jesus. He knows me completely.

And yet, even though He was able to see this chaos, fear, and need for control inside of me, He also saw the potential for beauty. Even at my worst moment, He did not withdraw His love. His love is unconditional.

Don't you care that I seem to be the only one doing everything?

My problem was in that one word, *doing*. I was so busy doing, that I could not take the time to listen to Jesus. He had taken the time to visit and spend time with me, and I was too busy to sit with Him. Mary understood how to be with Jesus, how to wait on Him. That made me envious, bitter, angry.

But then Jesus looked at me. "Martha, Martha." He said it slowly, looking right at me with compassion. Just hearing my name on His lips reminded me of so much. I remembered the very first time I heard Jesus speak in our synagogue. He had taught us from the prophet Isaiah.

Blessed are all who wait on Him.

I had learned what it meant to wait. It had been a difficult lesson over the months I had known Jesus. He had made us wait to see Lazarus raised from the dead. But what an amazing miracle that was to behold. Our grief was wiped away by the joy of that moment.

I had been at Jesus side when He spoke to us about what His Father was like and His mercy and forgiveness. I had seen Jesus take the time to talk to children while making the leaders of our village wait to speak with Him. I had seen Him touch the outcasts of society, the lepers, and heal them. He moved at a measured speed yet still accomplished everything He needed to do. He never fretted over anything. He never worried about what people thought of Him. He was at peace. Why couldn't I be more like Him?

Cast all your cares on Me...

Be still and know that I am God...

Blessed are all who wait on the Lord...

Those who wait on the Lord will renew their strength....

From that day on I tried to remember this lesson. Sometimes Mary would have to remind me. "Martha," she would say, "take some time to just listen today instead of getting all of the items on your list completed. Remember you're a human being not a human doing." We would laugh together as we did when we were children.

Take time to be still and listen as He calls your name.

Martha, Martha.

Hannah, Hannah.

Christine, Christine.

Be still and know that He is God. He cares for you. He sees your pain and struggles. He is with you always, while you are awake and while you are sleeping. He is your loving Father. Rest in Him.

6

Claudia

I am a woman mentioned very briefly in the pages of the Bible. You know me by a title, a very unflattering title. *The woman caught in adultery.* That is the way I am identified. My story is so short. You are not told anything about my life before or after that incident. I would like to open my life to you a little and try to give you a fuller picture of who I was before that event, and how an encounter with the Son of God changed me completely.

The event that marked me happened on a very dark night, I do remember that clearly. Asher had seen me earlier that week outside the temple. Asher is the name of the man with whom I was caught. He had once been my sweetheart; that was before our very wealthy neighbor, Simon, had arranged for him to marry his daughter, Milcah. Since Simon was a Pharisee, Asher's family was honored that he would be chosen as a suitable husband for Milcah. Even though there had been an understanding between Asher's parents and mine that we would be married, Asher and Milcah did indeed marry. Ours was the only family in our little section of town that was not invited to the glorious wedding.

I was angry and hurt, humiliated really. Asher had been my friend for as long as I had memories. Who could take his place? Certainly not the butcher's son, Shem, who hardly mumbled two words and had hands the size of Mama's largest bowl. Since Asher's wedding, he had been hinting about marriage to me every time I accompanied my mother to his father's shop. Just thinking about him made me shudder. Besides, he did not know me. We did not share any stories together.

Asher and I had shared so many adventures together as children. We were both the only children in our families and so had played together from the time we could walk. Shem could not finish my sentences as Asher could. Would he even get my sense of humor? Certainly, my parents never did quite understand my jokes, although they would try to smile. Sometimes I wondered if they simply thought I was like my father's older, unmarried sister who was a bit strange. Anyway, I have so much to share. I just needed you to know enough background to understand my story.

Since Asher's marriage, he had become quite an important man. Because of Simon, his father-in-law, he became one of the leaders in our area. This should have been a good thing, but it was not. His position and the power that came with it changed him in many ways, not very positive ways. For instance, power accentuated his weakness. He no longer had his own personality. He became more and more like his father-in-law each day. He did not speak or even walk the same way any longer. When he and Simon walked into the temple side by side, it was difficult to tell them apart. I was so very disappointed to see these changes in him. I thought I really knew him. What had happened to cause such changes?

It was during the Feast of the Tabernacles when we saw each other on the way home from the market. I was surprised that Asher even spoke to me. Since his marriage, we had not spoken. Milcah was always around and never allowed me to get within two feet of him. I guess I cannot blame her.

That day it appeared he had been waiting for me as I walked home. I wish I could say that I was not pleased that he was looking for me, waiting for me. But I was delighted. I missed him. The old Asher was back. He was smiling and had me laughing in minutes. He always knew just what to say to make me chuckle. After a few moments, he described how unhappy he was with Milcah. She was so critical and was a nag. She did not appreciate his sense of humor. She was not interested in talking with him about anything. He claimed that she was completely uninterested in him in any way. The only communication between them was when she criticized him. She constantly compared him to her father, he said.

"I should have married you, Claudia."

I could not believe he had spoken those words aloud. I felt a nervous laugh bubble up. I was happy but cautious at the same time. Honestly, so many different feelings and thoughts raced through my mind.

Milcah was not a good wife. I should have been the one that Asher married. It was what our families had assumed would happen. I had been suffering, and now I knew that Asher also suffered.

It was so good for my wounded pride to know that I would have been a better wife than Milcah. Before I could say a word, Asher pulled me into a narrow ally and inside his uncle's shop. This was a familiar place. We had come here many times throughout our childhoods. However on this visit, Asher's uncle was nowhere in sight. What were we doing here?

"I have missed you so much. Say you have missed me too."

Suddenly his arms were around me, and his lips were on mine.

I know what you are thinking, and you are right. I should have run out of there as fast as my legs could carry me. I should have pushed him away, screamed, anything. I did not even think of doing any of that at the time. It felt so good to have Asher back.

"We cannot stay here now as my uncle will be back soon. Meet me here tonight. I have been so lonely without you. I do not know what to do. You are the only person I can talk to about this. I am sorry to have kissed you. Please forgive me. It will not happen again. Just say you will come. I need you, Claudia. Please, promise me you will come."

His voice broke on the last word. He wiped tears from the corner of his eye. How could I say no to my best friend when he was so desperate? I fell for it: hook, line, and sinker.

That night, after my parents went to bed, I headed for the shop. I should have known better, and I guess deep down I knew what would happen that night. I chose not to listen to that small voice warning me to think about what I was doing. All I chose to think about was Asher's pitiful, pleading face. Actually, that's not really true. I also thought about how good it felt to be needed and to be chosen over the gloating Milcah.

I was there later that night, and you know what happened. However, I would like to share some important details. At a very indiscreet moment, several men burst into the room. I thought my heart would explode. I screamed. At first, I could not believe what was happening.

Asher did not have the same reaction. He rose slowly from my side.

"Asher, what is happening? Asher?" I tried to cover myself as I looked from his calm face into the excited, determined faces of the intruders.

He would not look at me. He bent to gather his robe and sandals and left me there. As he walked out of the room, one of the men patted his shoulder. It was Simon, his father-in-law. The group of jackals circled me. I was terrified.

It was almost dawn when my meeting with Asher was interrupted. The men who had entered the room were led by Simon and were all Pharisees and teachers of the law, most of whom I knew. They allowed me to cover myself with only a sheet. I could hardly think in those moments. What had just happened? Why was I being kept here by these men? What was going to happen to me? What would my family think when they heard what I had done?

I would never be able to show my face again in public. And where had Asher gone? Something was very wrong. Unfortunately, I was about to discover some of the answers to my many questions.

Just after dawn, the group of men dragged me out of the shop and pulled me towards the temple. It was the Sabbath. Surely, they would not take me to the temple wrapped in just a sheet. I pleaded with them, as I had been too shocked to do before. I began with a whisper, which they ignored. Soon I was sobbing and pleading. It did not take long for these men to drag me into the temple courts. By the time we arrived at the temple, my arm ached from the rough treatment. Simon was not gentle when he grabbed me. Even though it was early, already a small crowd had gathered. They were listening to the rabbi, Jesus. He had been teaching all week in the temple.

The Pharisees brought me right through the crowd and forced me to stand directly in front of Jesus who was seated before the listening crowd. I cannot begin to describe how ashamed and horrified I felt. Simon cleared his throat loudly in order to interrupt Jesus. Once he had everyone's attention, he spoke.

"Teacher, this woman was caught in the act of adultery. The law of Moses says she should be stoned. What do you say?"

The crowd was at my back, but I could feel their eyes on me. I shut my own eyes tightly. Was I hoping if I did that, the whole nightmare would go away? I was still weeping. My throat felt raw. I wished I could just disappear.

It was awfully quiet. I chanced a look at the rabbi seated in front of me. He had not answered the teachers of the law. His head was bowed, and He was writing in the dust at His feet. Why was He doing that? Did He not want to answer them? He wrote slowly with His finger.

I, even I, am He that blots out your transgressions for My own sake, and will remember your sins no more.

I read what He wrote and glanced sharply at Him. He raised His head and stared into my face as He rose slowly to His feet. Was He writing that for me? I looked at the men around me. They did not have any reaction to what Jesus had written. Had they even read it? They were becoming impatient waiting for His answer. The people were whispering, and I heard a few nervous laughs.

At that point, the Pharisees started once again to demand an answer to their question. "What do You say? Should we stone her right now? She is guilty. There are many witnesses."

Jesus was not hurried but took His time before giving His unusual answer.

"All right. Only let the one who is without sin throw the first stone."

I rubbed my arms as if I could feel the sharp edges of that first stone tearing into my flesh. Simon and his gang were not sure what to do with

Jesus' answer. The crowd was hushed waiting to see their reaction. I was not sure what my fate would be either.

Once again, Jesus stooped down and wrote in the dust at His feet. The Pharisees whispered among themselves.

Slowly, I began to understand what was happening. Simon and his group were trying to trap Jesus with this charade. If He contradicted the teaching of Moses, that would have caused Him terrible trouble. The people would feel betrayed by Him because He did not honor Moses, a great leader. If He called for the stoning of a woman, that would probably cause a different sort of trouble for Him and His followers.

I did not know everything about the law, but I did know that if anyone was to be stoned, then it should not just be me. Asher should also be tried, and if found guilty, then we both could be stoned, but not without a fair trial, not on the Sabbath. Besides, nothing like this had been done in years.

Asher.

Suddenly, I realized that this whole situation with him had been part of the plot. Asher had been involved with these men from the beginning. Had he really lured me into meeting him? Was that why he had been allowed to leave so quickly and without even a word of reproach? He had done this to me. He had manipulated me.

It was that thought that drove me to my knees right there in the dust. I began sobbing again. I could not help it. His betrayal was harder to suffer than the shame of standing in the temple wrapped in a sheet.

I did not hear or see each of my accusers as they walked away briskly, leaving me alone in the front of the group gathered around Jesus. I felt a soft touch on my hair. I flinched. Knowing that I had been so cruelly used made me angry, as I had never been angry before. When I lifted my head, I looked directly into Jesus' face.

"Where are your accusers? Didn't even one condemn you?" He spoke softly, kindly.

I realized that all of my tormentors had disappeared. "No Lord," I croaked, wiping the tears from my face. I hung my head, too exhausted and wounded to do anything else. Once again I noticed what was written in the dust.

To the Lord our God belong mercies and forgiveness.

Jesus spoke again as He gently laid His hand on my head. "Neither do I. Go and sin no more."

He placed both hands on my arms and helped me to my feet. I was free to go. I felt numb. I did not even look at anyone in the crowd. I stumbled out of the temple and did not stop running until I got to my house. I can only imagine the scene I caused.

My parents were aghast when I tumbled through the door. I could not tell them the tale for two days. I was too upset and did not leave the house. During those two days, I kept replaying the scene in my mind. First, I struggled to accept that Asher agreed and participated in this awful affair. This was very difficult for me to accept. But even more difficult was the fact that I had been so willing to compromise on all of the things that I claimed to believe, and commit adultery. I could hardly come to terms with the shame of what I had done. I had shamed my entire family, and everyone knew. I was sure of that because of the comments my parents had to endure when they did leave the house. I also kept thinking about those words written in the dust by Jesus.

I will blot out your transgressions.

To the Lord our God belong mercies and forgiveness.

I certainly needed forgiveness. I needed to learn more about Jesus. He said He did not condemn me, but He also said to sin no more. Was He saying He was able to forgive my sin? That would make Him equal with God. That was blasphemy.

At the very least, I knew I needed to thank Him for rescuing me from the clutches of the Pharisees. I needed to see Him again. This was the thought that gave me the courage to leave the security of my house a few days later and find Jesus.

I was so wrapped up in shawls that I am sure not even my own parents would have recognized me. I kept my head down as I walked to the temple, hoping Jesus was still there. As soon as I entered the outer courts, I knew He was there. A rather large crowd gathered around Him, and the Pharisees were huddled on the upper level walls watching and, no doubt, judging and plotting. I eased my way into a spot where I could hear what was being said. Unfortunately, I could not see Jesus, but I recognized His voice.

"Do not judge, and you will not be judged. Do not condemn, and you will not be condemned. Forgive and you shall be forgiven."

He spoke the words with such power, not just a powerful voice. The power I am talking about is the kind of power that reaches inside and brings about change. I don't know if that makes sense to you. But those few words were like water to my parched soul. Jesus had offered me mercy by refusing to condemn me right here just a few days previously. He had offered me forgiveness in front of the entire crowd gathered. I could feel the tears begin. I thought I had cried every tear available in my body, but now more flowed down my cheeks. I hurried out of the temple and back home. I did not want another public humiliation in the temple.

Later that night as I lay awake late, praying and thinking, another idea dawned on me. I had been forgiven for what I had done, but there was someone I needed to forgive.

No. I could not believe that anyone would think that I should offer him or the others forgiveness. I would never forgive Asher for his betrayal. He did not deserve it. Even my blessed mother had called him names I had never heard from her saintly lips before. No one would expect me to forgive any of those monsters.

Over the next several months, I slowly worked my way back into everyday life. Although, I would forever be known as a sinful woman in our village. I would never be able to find a husband, and my parents were disgraced. Somehow, in spite of the hardships, we managed. There were a few dear friends who remained faithful to my parents, but I know it was difficult for them. Many times I heard my father comforting my mother late at night as she cried.

We continued to hear stories about Jesus. He healed all kinds of diseases and even performed some of these miracles on the Sabbath. This further infuriated the Pharisees. No work was to be done on the Sabbath. How quickly they forgot that it was a Sabbath when they plotted to catch Asher and I together and tried to use me to trap Jesus with an impossible question.

I wish I could tell you that I was able to move on with life as though nothing had happened, but I did not. I became more and more bitter. The hatred I now felt for Asher and the teachers of the law, including Asher's father-in-law, was what I fed on day and night. I often would daydream of ways to expose the hypocrisy of Simon and his gang.

Many hours of my life were wasted this way. It took me to a very dark place. I was always angry. I played the role of victim so well that I almost forgot that no one forced me into that situation. I could have refused to meet with Asher. It was my choice to go. But I was able to bury those thoughts deep in my subconscious, until I heard Jesus' teaching the next time He was in the temple.

Once again He was seated, surrounded by a crowd. This time, with my parents, I was able to get to a place where I could see His face. His words, as always, were transformational.

"Come unto me all of you who are weary and I will give you rest. I am the Light of the world. Walk in the Light. You who claim to have the Light and yet hate your brother, you are a liar.

Forgive and be merciful just as God has forgiven and been merciful to you. You are not sure you can forgive because the hurt is too great. Alone you can do nothing, this is true. But in your weakness, that is when you will be strong because you will learn to rely on My power. You can do anything with My power, with God's power.

Listen to my words. Judge not. Condemn not. Forgive as you have been forgiven. Love your enemies and pray for those who persecute you. Blessed are the merciful, for they shall receive mercy."

At the end of Jesus' teaching, the crowd surged forward. I stood in the same spot until I felt my father's hands pull me toward the gate. Jesus' words had pierced the darkness of my heart. I had been forgiven, but I had not shown forgiveness. I did not love my enemies. I hated them and longed to humiliate them. I was certainly not merciful. I was not walking in the Light.

I was weary of playing the victim. I was weary of this darkness that had grown in my heart. I was weary of life. This was not the way to live. But how did I change it all? I could not go back and change what had happened. I could not simply say I forgave the monsters that had done this to me. And how did I forgive myself for what I had done?

I wanted to follow Jesus' teaching. Every time I was in His presence, I felt free and clean, loved and understood. I did not feel the heavy shame that I lived with every day. I did not feel the intense hatred that had overtaken my life. How did I go about letting go of those things and allowing myself to experience this freedom each day?

Had Jesus spoken those words just for me? I realized that I had been so very wrong over the last few months. I had become like the very people I despised. I was vengeful and condemning. If I had the power of the Pharisees, I would punish my enemies severely for the wrongs they inflicted on me. Isn't that what I envisioned each night when sleep would not come to me? I wanted the world to know what hypocrites Simon and his minions were. Yet, I was realizing what a hypocrite I was.

On that awful early morning, when I stood wrapped in just a sheet and my shame in front of Jesus, He said, "Go and sin no more."

Of course, I thought He was speaking about my sin of adultery, but today I understood that there was more to His charge than I grasped at the time. Every day since then, I had filled my life with sin. Oh, I did not commit adultery or any of those big, outwardly obvious sins, but what about my judgment, hatred, jealousy, anger, and selfishness? The list could go on. Suddenly, I was overwhelmed by the extent of God's forgiveness. His mercy toward me was so amazing. I had been forgiven of so much. How could I continue to hold on to my hatred for Asher and the other men involved in the plot? I needed to let it go. I knew I could not do this alone. I needed to ask God to help me.

I rushed to my room after returning from the temple and knelt. I prayed differently than ever before. Instead of reminding God what a victim I was and what should be done to make things right for me, I admitted my own sin. I took responsibility for my actions and thanked God for His forgiveness. Then I asked Him to help me to do what I thought He was asking me to do, forgive Asher and the other men.

I confessed my hatred for them and my anger for all of the pain they had brought into my life and the lives of my dear parents. I told Him that I did not want to let it all go, but I knew He wanted me to do so.

"You will have to make this happen. I cannot do this without You, Lord."

It may sound like a silly and simplistic prayer to you, but it was the most honest prayer I had ever prayed. My feelings did not change in that instant, as I wanted. However, the darkness and anger that had become my daily companions started to fade away over the next several days and weeks. The light of Jesus' words filled my soul. My weariness melted away a bit more each day. I desperately wanted to let Jesus know how grateful I was for His patience and His forgiveness, now that I fully understood how much I had been forgiven.

A few weeks later, I heard from a neighbor that Jesus had been invited to eat at Simon's house that evening. I knew that nothing would stop me from going there and letting Jesus know how His mercy and forgiveness had rescued me from a life filled with darkness. I was so desperate to see Jesus that I was willing to risk being thrown into the street. I would not put it past Simon or his daughter to have me tossed out by a servant since I had not been invited to the dinner. I didn't care. I wanted to do something to show my gratitude.

I used some of the money I had been saving for many years to purchase an alabaster jar of costly myrrh, which I would use to anoint Jesus' head to show the respect I had for Him. I obviously did not take the time to really craft a careful plan. How was I going to be the one to greet Jesus at the door and anoint His head? This was the job of the host. Sometimes, one of the more important servants would be given this honor if the guest list were large. I guess I did not think about that part of my plan.

I arrived at Simon's house just after Jesus and His disciples. Because of the large number of them entering at the same time, I was able to slip inside unrecognized. There was no servant at the door washing the feet of the guests or anointing their heads. Simon was not at the door either to greet his guests.

I stayed out of the way until the meal began. I was feeling completely overwhelmed with gratitude for my forgiveness. I knew that Jesus had been speaking to me that day in the temple weeks earlier. Did He know that I had asked God to help me to forgive Asher, Simon, and the other Pharisees involved in the plot against me? I wished I could talk with Him and tell Him about the impact His words had wrought on my life.

About five minutes into the meal, the two men standing in front of me moved outside the room. Jesus was reclining before me eating His meal. Something inside of me broke when I saw Him. I moved forward uncaring of all around me and knelt at Jesus feet. I began to weep with deep gratitude, and my tears fell onto His dusty feet. The more I thought about the hatred I had allowed to fester in my heart, the harder I cried. I used my hair to wipe His dirty feet. Shouldn't a servant have washed His feet when He entered? Finally, I pulled the jar of myrrh from my cloak, broke it open, and poured it onto His feet. This act, though it might sound outrageous, seemed like the right thing to do at the time. As the scent of myrrh filled the room, the sounds of conversation ceased. I was unconcerned.

If I could have read their minds, I would have known that the guests were horrified that I dared to enter this house. Simon was smirking, probably thinking that if Jesus really were the Son of God, He would have known who I was. He would have remembered me, surely. Of course, I had an idea of the commotion my presence would cause when I planned this, but at that moment it was the last thing on my mind. However, it was as if Jesus could read Simon's mind.

"Simon, I have something to tell you."

"Tell me, Teacher." So Jesus told this parable.

"Two men owed money to a moneylender. One owed 500 denarii and one owed 50. Neither of them had the money to pay him back so he cancelled both debts. Now which of them will love him more?"

"I suppose the one who owed the most money," Simon replied.

Jesus smiled and congratulated him, "You have judged correctly." Simon smiled broadly, looking pleased for his correct answer. His gloating was cut short by Jesus' next words.

"Do you see this woman?" Every eye in the room now focused on me. Of course they all saw me. A weeping woman holding a man's feet at the dinner table is quite hard to miss. Jesus surely did have a sense of humor.

"You did not give Me any water to wash My feet or greet Me with a kiss, but she has not stopped kissing My feet and washing them with her tears, drying them with her hair. You did not honor Me by anointing My head with oil, but she has poured perfume on My feet. She has honored Me with all she has. Therefore I tell you, her many sins are forgiven for she loved much. But he who has not seen his need for forgiveness, loves little."

Then Jesus fixed His gaze on me. I smiled. "Woman, your sins are forgiven. Your faith has saved you. Go in peace."

Those three short sentences were a precious gift. At those words, the uncomfortable quiet that had filled the room like a fog, exploded into heated discussion.

"Who does He think He is?"

"Only God can forgive sin."

"What an insult to Simon."

Even in the midst of the chaos, serenity poured into my soul. I could not stop smiling. A lightness I had not experienced since childhood allowed me to ignore all of the hard stares, the oaths directed toward me, and the disgust. I had not confessed my sins of bitterness and hatred to Jesus tonight, but somehow I understood that He knew just what my sins were when He spoke those words.

Your sins are forgiven.

What beautiful words those were. They set me free from darkness so overwhelming that it was destroying my life. There was not a thing that anyone in that room could do to dim the joy I felt. Simon's frown, embarrassment, and anger could not touch me.

Even though I will always be known to some as the woman caught in adultery, I do not allow it to bother me because it reminds me of Jesus'

forgiveness, God's forgiveness. It reminds me to extend that same forgiveness to others and not be too hasty to judge.

I did leave in peace that night from Simon's house. It is a peace that
has never left me even through many difficulties. I continued to try to
walk in the Light, to love others and be merciful to them, even when
they were unkind or cruel. It has not been easy. But God has been with
me each day, each moment.

7

Zacchaeus's Wife

What did my husband just say? Did he actually promise to give away all of our money? Surely, I must have misheard him because of one too many goblets of wine.

When I heard Zacchaeus offer to give away our money, I was stunned. I had become very accustomed to the luxuries that our money could buy. We were able to own slaves who took care of everything for us. I wore the richest fabrics and had many beautiful jewels. Our house was one of the loveliest in the city. Certainly, the Jews hated us and kept themselves apart from us. This did not bother me at all. I was Roman by birth. I did not care about the Jews, either. Zacchaeus was a Jew, but he was different. He did not follow all of the silly rules and laws. Because he was a tax collector for the Romans, he had turned his back on his Jewish heritage and was hated by the Jews. Many ugly stories were told about his collection of taxes. Most of them were true.

However, no one knew how much these stories bothered Zacchaeus, except me. I knew how much he wanted to fit in and how much he missed his family who no longer spoke to him. He did not participate in the synagogue days and festivals of his people. However, he was always a bit more downcast on those special days. For years after our marriage, I longed to help him forget about all of these constraining rules and legalisms, but I was not able to do so. What kind of religion showered so much guilt upon the heads of its followers? Zac was better off without that pressure in his life. There were too many of these rules to follow.

Over the past couple of years, I had become irritated with him over this issue. How many more years was he going to mourn for something he could not have? Had he not made his own choice to work for the government? Had he not become a very wealthy man doing his job? Did he not have the respect of the local rulers? What more could he really need?

Years ago we met because he came to work for my father when he was a young man. I did not know all the details. All I remember is that my father hired Zacchaeus when I was about 10 years old. Zac was a rather short man, much shorter than my father or any other man I knew. He had a stern expression on his face most of the time and was very intense. At dinner, my father often told stories about how smart Zac was in business.

Zac was amazing at increasing the profits. Over the months and years, Father trusted Zac to run more and more of the business. Zac took my family's small enterprise and made it quite prosperous. We were not wealthy, but we no longer had to worry about surviving. This made my father very happy. So two years later, when Zac asked my father for permission to marry me, the immediate answer was yes.

In Roman culture it was customary for parents to ask their daughters if they wanted to accept a suitor's offer. I was eager for the match with Zac. Even though he was not a handsome man and was a head shorter than me, I knew he would be a good husband. He would be able to provide well for me. I did long to have lots of lovely things like some of the beautifully dressed ladies I saw. I often dreamed of what it would be like to be ridiculously wealthy. Happily, it was not very long after my marriage, when those dreams started to come true.

I was surprised one morning when Zac sheepishly announced that he was going to the synagogue to hear a new rabbi. Zac had never attended synagogue since I had known him. He would have been considered unclean and unwelcome in the synagogue, if for no other reason than because he was married to a Gentile.

"Are you playing a joke on me, Zac? Why would you want to go there?" He started to explain that there was a new and somewhat un-orthodox rabbi who was going to be teaching there.

"He has captured the imaginations of the people. Some say that He is the Messiah that we have waited on for so long. He has been saying and doing amazing things in the city. Most of what I have heard, I do not believe, but I think it would be fun to hear Him for myself. It will be entertaining, at least."

This new rabbi had been teaching in the temple for several days now. The people talked about him incessantly. The only reason I could think of that would make Zac willing to enter the synagogue was because he did not want to be left out of all the conversations people were having about the rabbi, Jesus. It seemed as though He was lauded by Jews and Gentiles alike. Some of Zac's associates said Jesus claimed that God did not have favorites, that He treated all people the same, that there was neither Jew nor Greek, male or female in the kingdom of God. This was certainly radical teaching. I wondered what the established Jewish leaders thought about that. One of the morning prayers of the Pharisees was something like, "God I thank You that I am not a woman."

When Zac returned from the synagogue later that day, he was full of stories about his experience. I had not seen him so excited since perhaps our wedding. He told me about what Jesus taught at the temple that day. Apparently, He taught by telling a parable seemingly designed to shame the Pharisees. That made Zacchaeus quite happy, as they were his biggest enemies. It was not uncommon for them to stir up trouble for him when-ever they could. When I heard the description of the Pharisees' discom-fort, I wanted to hear the story Jesus told. Zacchaeus was eager to tell me.

Jesus started by saying He was telling this story to those who were too confident in their own righteousness. That one statement captured everyone's attention. Everyone knew who claimed to be completely righ-teous: the Pharisees. Then He described two different men who went up to the temple to pray. One was a Pharisee and the other a tax collector.

The Pharisee stood in a prominent place in the temple, spread his arms, and raised his eyes to heaven. In a loud voice, he stated, "God, I thank you that I am not like other people—robbers, evildoers, adulterers—or even like this tax collector." Then Jesus continued by quoting the Pharisee to say that he fasted twice a week and gave a tenth of all he owned away.

This was an accurate description of what Pharisees normally did. It was not unusual in any way. They always loved to be noticed for all of their good deeds. But I happened to know of many deeds committed by the Pharisees that were far less than good. Since I was Roman and not Jewish, the Pharisees did not care about impressing me. They did not feel as though they had to put on their holy persona for us. There had been many Pharisees over the years, who had done business with my father, and cheated him out of his fees. I wondered what the good Jewish folk at the synagogue would think if they knew about that?

The first part of this story was no surprise to me. This was what happened each day in the temple as far as I knew. It was the second part of the story that was so shocking. In this part Jesus told the story of the tax collector. He too entered the synagogue to pray. Unlike the Pharisee, he chose a dark corner of the temple to stand. He did not want to draw attention to himself. He did not even raise his eyes to the heavens, but instead beat his breast and wept. His words were moaned. "God, have mercy on me, a sinner."

Jesus stunned the gathered crowd by His next statement. They were not prepared for what He was about to say. How could they be? They had never heard anything like this before.

Jesus paused for a moment. "I tell you that this man, the tax collector, went home justified by God. For all who exalt themselves will be humbled, and those who humble themselves will be exalted."

I could not believe that a rabbi had said this. Zacchaeus was so excited as he told me the story. He felt as though Jesus had known he was going to be there that day and had told this story just for him. This was not possible of course, but I did not want to argue with my husband. He was convinced that Jesus was telling him that he could be forgiven for any of his past misdeeds.

I was not sure exactly why my husband felt he needed to be forgiven. He was a good businessman. He was a good husband. What did it mean to be a sinner, anyway?

The Pharisees present had been outraged. They had caused quite a commotion before leaving in a huff. Many of the people in the temple had been in shock. They could not imagine ever going against the powerful Pharisees. They knew how much trouble they would cause if they ever tried to question them or stand up to them.

I was not surprised to hear that there had been a problem. This rabbi had better be careful. If He continued to speak out against the Pharisees, He would find Himself in a lot of trouble. He would not last long in the city.

I was not sure that I really understood the story fully, but I was so glad to hear that someone was willing to challenge these hypocrites. I was intrigued by the idea that a rabbi would choose to honor a tax collector over a Pharisee. What kind of rabbi was this? I decided that maybe I needed to hear this rabbi for myself. What fun it would be to watch the faces of the smug Pharisees as Jesus called them on their hypocrisy.

It was just a few days later when Zacchaeus heard that Jesus would be visiting our area. He raced out of the house toward the town square. He left so quickly that I did not even have the chance to go along with him.

It wasn't more than a couple of hours later when one of the servants came into the room with news that shocked me into action. He said that Jesus and all of His disciples would be arriving at the house shortly and would be staying with us. Zacchaeus had invited them all and wanted me to organize a dinner in their honor. I could not believe it. For one thing, there was no way a true rabbi would enter the house of a tax collector. For another, what was Zac thinking to invite a large group of people to dinner when nothing was prepared?

Usually dinner invitations were issued many days before an event. Then a second invitation was sent on the day of the dinner, including the time of the meal. Dinners required a lot of preparation in our day. I had to borrow supplies from several neighbors in order to come up with the food necessary to feed such a large group. It was an exhausting several hours of preparation.

By the time the huge group of men arrived at the house, I had worked myself into quite a state. Even though I was excited to meet the rabbi who had humiliated the Pharisees with His teaching, I was overwhelmed with the work of preparing for this unplanned dinner. Still, I was eager to meet this obviously powerful man.

I must admit that I was not impressed with Jesus when He entered our house. His clothing was rough and dusty. He was no more important-looking than any of His followers. They all looked quite common and even a bit dirty. I am not sure what I was expecting, but it was not an average-looking, travel-weary Jew. Even His features were unremarkable. After all of the work I had put into this meal, I was terribly disappointed with our guests. I had been hoping to meet a dynamic man, a powerful man who might even be helpful to us in the city. Jesus was definitely not such a man.

The hastily prepared meal was served and enjoyed by our very hungry guests. I don't think there was a morsel of food left over. Throughout the meal, there was a lot of laughter and conversation. I found myself being sucked into the good mood a few times. I was finally beginning to relax. The wine might have had something to do with that. However, I also realized that the dinner had gone smoothly, and everyone had enjoyed the meal. Unfortunately, I was about to have the biggest shock of my life. Toward the end of the evening, Jesus held up His hand for silence. He spoke quietly but clearly.

"Do not store up for yourselves treasures on earth, where moths and vermin destroy, and where thieves break in and steal. But store up for yourselves treasures in heaven, where moths and vermin do not destroy, and where thieves do not break in and steal. For where your treasure is, there your heart will be also.

No one can serve two masters. Either you will hate the one and love the other, or you will be devoted to the one and despise the other. You cannot serve both God and money."

Zacchaeus was listening intently as Jesus spoke.

"Therefore I tell you, do not worry about your life, what you will eat or drink; or about your body, what you will wear. Is not life more than food, and the body more than clothes? Look at the birds of the air; they do not sow or reap or store away in barns, and yet your heavenly Father feeds them. Are you not much more valuable than they? Can any one of you by worrying add a single hour to your life? And why do you worry about clothes? See how the flowers of the field grow. They do not labor or spin. Yet I tell you that not even Solomon, in all his splendor, was dressed like one of these. If that is how God clothes the grass of the field, which is here today and tomorrow, is thrown into the fire, will He not much more clothe you?"

At this point Jesus turned to Zacchaeus and put His hand on his shoulder. With a smile on His face, He spoke. "So do not worry about what you will eat, drink, or wear. For the pagans run after all these things, and your heavenly Father knows that you need them. But seek first His kingdom and His righteousness, and all these things will be given to you as well. Therefore do not worry about tomorrow, for tomorrow will worry about itself. Each day has enough trouble of its own, doesn't it?"

Jesus finished His speech and laughed heartily. There was loud clapping. The disciples were talking together with Zac, laughing, and patting each other on the back. They had enjoyed Jesus' mini-sermon. I did not have the same reaction. I felt as though He had been trying to insult me. He had condemned me for my love of pretty clothes and grand things. It was certainly very rude of Him to come into my home, enjoy my hospitality, and then insult me for it. The relaxing effects of the good wine wore off very quickly.

Suddenly my husband surged to his feet. I was sure he was about to chastise Jesus for His rude comments about chasing after money. Zac could be very authoritative when necessary. I had seen him deal masterfully with many people over the years. I straightened in my seat at the opposite end of the table. Zac brushed a hand across his eyes as he stood to his feet. He clapped his hands to get everyone's attention before speaking. It took a while for all of the different conversations to come to an end. Zacchaeus's face was flushed as he started speaking. In a shaky voice he began.

"Today has been the most amazing day of my life. I cannot believe that I have been welcomed into this band of brothers. This day has changed my life."

Well, I could hardly listen after the first statement. Zac had always claimed that the best day of his life was our wedding day. I could feel the heat in my cheeks. Was he trying to humiliate me? Wasn't he going to stand up to Jesus on my behalf? Was he going to let this vagabond insult me at my own table?

Zac continued speaking and made several pledges. His first promise was to repay people twice what he had collected from them in taxes. Our guests cheered after he made this claim. Cups were raised and Zacchaeus was congratulated by several of our guests. I did not feel like cheering. I wanted to throttle him. He had obviously had too much to drink.

Tax collectors were given the freedom to collect whatever taxes they wished from the community. The government did not care as long as they received the required amount. It was normal for collectors to demand a bit extra so that they could keep the money and make a profit. This was considered good business practice. This was one of the reasons we had become so wealthy. Before I could think too long about this outrageous statement, Zac made another insane promise.

"I will give away half of the rest of my money to the needy."

I could never have imagined that this day, which had begun with a harmless adventure, would end with us in poverty. I felt sick to my stomach. We would have nothing left if Zac followed through on these promises. Jesus and all of His rowdy friends seemed pleased. There were shouts of approval and clapping, more cheers.

What kind of sorcery had Jesus worked on my husband? A few words about not serving money, and he was willing to throw away everything he had worked so hard to earn over the last several years. What would happen when we had no money to buy food or clothes? Would these men come and help us then? Would their God buy us food? It was fine to talk about not worrying about money until the time came when you had none. Then the real worrying would begin.

Jesus stood and raised His hands for silence once again. He put His arm around Zac's shoulder before speaking. "Today salvation has come to this house, because this man, too, is a son of Abraham. For the Son of Man came to seek and to save what was lost."

Zac was clearly moved and raised his cup in a toast. I could not remain at the table any longer. I fled before I embarrassed myself by screaming out my rage.

We had been hearing stories about Jesus for some time. Most of the stories that Zac and I had heard seemed ridiculous. No one could really heal lepers or cripples. No one could turn water into wine. Zac and I had laughed about that story. We would have been pleased if Jesus had done that for us. We would have gathered all of the water our jars could hold if He would have been willing to make the wine. He certainly did not offer to make any wine at dinner tonight.

What had Jesus said to Zacchaeus to make him think he must give away our money? Where would we live? What would we do? Was Zac thinking that he would no longer work for the Romans? I wanted to ask these questions immediately. However, I needed to wait for our guests to leave to get Zac alone and interrogate him. I paced around my room ranting to myself. I would get to the bottom of this later. Zac would surely come to his senses. He must have had too much wine, and was not thinking clearly.

Jesus was obviously a con man looking to steal our money and live comfortably from the profits. Most of the men who were traveling in His group were uneducated. Some of them smelled like they had been on the road for too many days. These were not men to be trusted. Surely, I would be able to convince Zac of this in the morning when the effects of tonight's wine had worn off and the cheering men were not around. I would help him to be sensible. Isn't that what wives were meant to do for their husbands?

By the time the group left our house, I had myself convinced that this was all a simple misunderstanding. Zac was surely not serious about what he had claimed during dinner. I was in for another shock when I finally had the opportunity to speak with him quietly the following day.

"You cannot be serious about giving away all of our fine possessions and all the money you have worked so hard to save."

Zac placed his hands on my shoulders, looked into my eyes, and smiled. He started at the beginning of his story, the day he went to the synagogue to hear the rabbi speak. Zac had not told me how deeply that one story had impacted him over the following days. We had laughed about those silly Pharisees at dinner. I thought that was the end of it. But it was only the beginning for Zacchaeus.

He had been filled with hope after hearing the parable. He saw himself in the parable. He was that tax collector. Even though they had never met, he felt Jesus was talking to him when describing the tax gatherer in His story. Zac wanted to believe the story might be for him. Over the next few days, Zac kept thinking about what it would look like for him to repent as the man in the story had done. He claimed he could not stop thinking about that question or about Jesus.

"Jesus was letting me know that I could be forgiven, Rona."

It broke my heart to see how much Zac wanted that to be true. He felt so inadequate. Even though he was a giant in finances, he could never come to terms with the fact that he was an outcast from his own people. No matter how hard he tried, he could not let that go.

On the day he had gone to see Jesus and brought Him back to our house, Zac had climbed the tall sycamore tree in the center of town. Since he was so short, he could not see Jesus in the crowd as He was walking by. He knew that people would make fun of him if they saw him in the tree. Yet, he endured the hoots and slurs. He did not care as long as he was able to get a look at Jesus again. Just as the crowd crossed the town square, Jesus stopped. He stood still for a moment. Then He looked up into the tree and spoke Zac's name.

"Zacchaeus, come on down from there. You are just the friend I have been looking for today. We would love to come to your house for dinner this very day. Thank you for the kind invitation."

He then waited for Zac to climb all the way down from his perch. At first, Zac was embarrassed being singled out from the crowd. All of the people in town knew who and what he was. The crowd was dumbfounded.

For a moment they were in shock, but as Zac climbed down from the tree branch, people started to talk. What they mumbled was not very flattering.

Not only did Jesus announce to everyone that He was going to the house of the local, hated, tax collector, but He had called him a friend. When Zac told me about that moment, I wished I had been there.

Zac spent the rest of the day with Jesus as He walked through the area visiting with the people. At one point, He healed a woman who had some sort of bleeding disease. Zac wasn't sure if Jesus had meant to do this. The woman had apparently been healed simply by reaching out and touching Jesus' garment as He walked by her.

"It was amazing, Rona. This old, feeble woman just touched the hem of His tunic as He passed by. There were so many people all around us, bumping into us at times. Yet, He knew the moment she touched Him. He stopped and asked who touched Him. Of course, we did not know what to say since so many people were pressed together."

But Zac said that this woman stepped forward and admitted to reaching out to Jesus in order to receive healing. "He can heal without even touching someone. It is amazing."

He also saw Jesus stop to talk and play with a group of children who were enjoying a game. The largest disciple, a fisherman named Peter, tried to get Jesus to move on, but Jesus did not listen to him. Instead, Jesus reprimanded Peter, saying that the kingdom of God belonged to the children. Zac was most assuredly intrigued by these experiences.

"There is one thing I know for sure, Rona," he whispered. "This is no ordinary man. This must be the Messiah of Israel. This is the One of whom the Scriptures have prophesied. I know it."

This was the first time I had ever heard Zac talk about the Jewish faith. It scared me. I was an outsider. When I confessed this, he took my hand.

"You can come to follow Jesus, Rona. It does not matter if you were born a Jew or Roman. Jesus has even healed a Roman soldier's daughter. He does not seem to care if you are a descendant of Abraham or not. He says that we must only love God, and love and serve our fellow man.

That is the way for us to enter the kingdom of God. He says forgiveness is ours if we ask for it. We do not need to earn our way into God's love, just accept Him. I have pledged to follow Jesus. I must do this. I want you with me."

Even though it sounded crazy to me, what could I say to my dear husband? For so long, he had been an outcast, a joke. He had endured mockery and hatred. Now here was Jesus offering friendship, hope, and salvation.

But the cost was great. I did not want to give up all of the things I had grown accustomed to enjoying. I did not want to obey all of the complicated laws of the Jewish faith. I did not want to have to worry about my next meal. I did not want to change my lifestyle for this rabbi.

My only other option would be to return to my father's house.

I would have to make a decision. Could I really seek God's Kingdom first and not worry about the wealth I had come to enjoy and rely on?

Would I follow Jesus with my husband?

8

Pontius Pilate's Wife

How would you like it if your husband was one of the most hated men in all the world? Of course, I know your answer. It is a silly question, really. My husband was not always the man you know about from your reading. When I met him, he was handsome, dynamic, driven and goal-oriented. He wanted to make a difference in the world. Sometimes, people get lost along the way.

He was one of those people who succumbed to the insanity of the Roman machine and could not turn back even when he knew what he was doing was a travesty of justice. He tried his best, but he felt he was without options. He was to pay the ultimate price for his lack of integrity throughout the years. Isn't it funny that we think we can get away with compromises until they catch up with us one day and demand payment? This is what happened to my husband.

My husband had been prefect in Judea for many years when we started to hear the name of Jesus mentioned in regards to civilian unrest in the district. Apparently, the rabble was quite intrigued with Jesus and His teaching. Everywhere He went, great crowds followed. The stories that filtered back to us were exaggerations, obviously. They told of this unimportant Galilean healing lepers, curing strange diseases, giving a blind man back his sight by rubbing mud and spit on his eyes, and feeding thousands of people using only a young boy's lunch. These were certainly not very believable stories.

However, there were some stories that concerned my husband. The people claimed that this man was the new leader of the Jews, their King. This threat could no longer be ignored. No one could take the place of Caesar. My husband knew that he had to do something about this man, Jesus. If news of these claims reached Caesar's ears, my husband could face disastrous consequences.

One of my maids, who was a Jew, went to hear Jesus, speak and returned very excited indeed. I questioned her about her experience. I was quite intrigued. It had been a while since anything this exciting had happened in the area. Jesus was providing some much-needed drama in my painfully humdrum life. After my maid's description of what she had seen and heard, I made a decision. I would dress as a Jew, go out into the streets with her, and see what was happening for myself. I would be entertained by a wonderful adventure that I could share with our friends and future guests. What fun it would be.

Jesus was supposed to be in town for a few days according to my maid. She knew where to look for Him. She thought He might be close to the synagogue. Apparently He had been there teaching for a couple of days.

After donning the rather unattractive clothes of the Hebrews, we set off to find our adventure. As we turned a corner in the narrow streets, we stumbled upon a large, rough-looking crowd. They all were craning their necks to see something that was happening up ahead. I found myself wishing that I had travelled with my usual guard so that I could move to the front of the crowd and have the best view. However, just at that moment, an odd thing happened. A narrow passageway opened in the midst of the mob and beckoned for us to walk through. Without speaking to each other, we made our way easily through the jostling, smelly throng of people. It wasn't long before I found myself standing right in front of the drama unfolding. My unusual journey had brought me into one of the small rough homes in the village.

Many of the Pharisees, who I knew because they often came to speak to my husband, were standing at the front of the crowd just inside the open door of the home. These supposedly holy men often came to discuss ways to keep the rabble of Jerusalem under control. There were many deals made over the years between the city leaders and my husband. It would be interesting to see what the locals would do if they knew how involved their leaders were in keeping them under control. Of course, the Pharisees told themselves they were doing it all for the good of the people. But, they were really just trying to protect themselves and their place of honor and respect in the local community. If they saw me, they would recognize me immediately. I was careful to make sure that the hood of my disguise covered most of my face. I angled my body away from their eyes. Fortunately, they were completely focused on the man who was standing at the center of the shabby room. Anger was radiating from them. Their bodies were rigid, and I thought that Ciaphus might actually crack his teeth because he was clenching them so tightly.

Was this Jesus? Why were they so angry? What had happened?

Just as Antipas, a leader of the Pharisees, was about to ask Jesus a question, some dust, then large portions of the roofing material, started to fall from above. Many in the crowd were getting covered with the falling dust. Before too long, the entire crowd was no longer focused on Jesus. We were all looking up at the falling roof. Large chunks of tile, mud and straw were raining down. We heard voices raised in excitement and what sounded like directions being given. It was quite a moment of confusion. I was very interested to see what was going to happen next.

As the hole in the roof opened, I noticed three or four young men peering down on us. Their faces were flushed, and they looked slightly abashed as if they knew how horrified all of us were at their crazy intrusion into this moment. When they spied the Pharisees below them, they physically pulled back from the opening. I could hear some furious whispering. We all craned our necks to see what might happen next. Anitpas raised his voice. "What is going on up there? What do you think you are doing here? Don't you realize you are intruding? Who are you? Show yourselves immediately."

One young man's face appeared in the opening for a moment. His face was set in determination. No matter what the cost, he knew he was going to accomplish the task he had set out to do. He disappeared once again, and his face was replaced with the bottom of a dirty mat. Slowly and carefully, the bedding was lowered from the roof. The crowd leaned forward eager to see what was happening. I took my eyes from the scene for a moment and chanced a look at Jesus.

He stood completely still. He seemed to be looking through the ceiling and seeing the men who were lowering the stretcher into the crowd. As people around Him moved a bit to allow the six-foot litter to settle on the ground, Jesus stood calmly in place. As if choreographed, it settled just at His feet. The faces once again appeared in the opening, staring down at the man lying on blankets at the feet of Jesus. They looked from his pained, embarrassed eyes into the eyes of Jesus. Perspiration beaded on their foreheads after the labor of using the crude ropes to lower this cripple to the feet of Jesus. There was pleading in their expressions.

Jesus did not speak for several moments. The crowd and even the Pharisees said nothing, as I think we were all at a loss for words. None of us had ever experienced anything like this. Quietly, a few people behind me started whispering.

"Isn't that Joseph, the son of Joshua? He has been ill since the day he was born. Such a burden to his parents, he is."

"He ought to be ashamed pulling such a stunt."

"You can just bet that his cousin, Cephas, is in on this caper. That young man is always getting into trouble in the village."

The whispers ended when Jesus nodded to the young men above and focused on the man at His feet. He spoke directly to him. "Friend, your sins are forgiven."

This one statement brought outraged gasps from the scribes and Pharisees who were in attendance. They were even angrier now than when I had entered the house. I could tell that several of them wanted to respond to what had been spoken. Instead, they pursed their lips, and

I promise, it looked as though steam was about to come from Ciaphus's ears.

I am guessing that they were thinking about what it meant that Jesus had told the man his sins were forgiven. Since I had done some studying of the Jewish beliefs over the past couple of years, I knew that one thing was very clearly stated in their holy writings. Only God could forgive sins. That was the whole point of their provincial religion. It was the reason the temple was central to them. Only there could the priests perform the regimented ceremonies that brought them forgiveness.

What did Jesus mean by what He said? Although His statement did not cause the anger in me that it did in the Jewish leaders, it did make me wonder about His words. Was Jesus taunting the leaders? What kind of dangerous game was He playing? He had to know that it was not smart or safe to vex these powerful men. Did He know that they had my husband's ear and could make His life very unpleasant? No one spoke against Caesar or the Jewish God.

As if reading their minds and mine, Jesus inhaled deeply and looked around the room. He looked into the eyes of each of the present leaders before speaking again. "Why are you thinking these things in your hearts? Is it easier for Me to say that this man's sins are forgiven, or to tell him to get up and walk? But I want you to know that the Son of Man has authority on earth to forgive sins."

Had Jesus just claimed to be God? Had He meant to say that? Had He been drinking this early in the day? What could He mean?

At that moment, Jesus turned again to the paralyzed man. He stooped down to the man and reached out to touch his face. He gently brushed the pale cheek while smiling at him. Then with great gentleness, He whispered, "I tell you, get up, take your mat, and go home."

As Jesus slowly stood to His feet, we all watched in silence. There was a groan from the man, not of agony, but of accomplishment. The covers over his legs began to move. It looked as though his obviously shriveled legs were growing. The man's face registered shock, disbelief, and finally, a hopeful joy. He gingerly raised his head from the mat. His limp hair hung almost to his shoulders. He trembled with the effort it took to sit up. He appeared dizzy for a moment. Then like a sunrise, a smile spread across his face. Energy pulsed from his once fragile body. He reached out his scrawny arm and threw back the blanket from his legs. Those of us watching at the front of the crowd gasped aloud. His feet, which were not covered in shoes, looked strong and young. It sounds odd to say, but that is what I thought. They looked as though they belonged to a robust, young soldier. He pulled himself to his knees and bowed his head before Jesus. His shoulders started to shake, and those of us close could hear his weeping. Jesus simply pulled the young man's shoulders into His body and comforted him. It was such an intimate embrace. It was a moment of pure love. I am sure I have never seen such real emotion expressed between two people before. I found myself wishing it were me that Jesus was holding and loving.

The young man did not remain on his knees for long. He looked up from his weeping, wiped his eyes with the back of his hand, and with a loud shout, jumped to his feet. He swayed unevenly for a moment, then raised his eyes to his friends who were still peering down at the scene from the opened tile roof. He jumped up as if he was trying to reach them and yelled again. They started shouting and praising God loudly. We could hear them scrambling down from the roof, likely on their way to try to reach their friend. Once again, he turned back to Jesus and reached out to Him. He hugged Him for a moment, stepped back, and nodded with the biggest smile on his face. He bent to roll up his dirty mat, hoisted it onto his head and turned to make his way out of the house. The packed crowd made a path for him to exit. All eyes followed him as he walked or should I say strutted from the dwelling.

What had just happened? If I had not heard the conversations whispered around me, I might have thought that this was an elaborate hoax enacted to bring some attention to Jesus. But why would He offend the Pharisees like this? And, this was obviously a young man well-known in the area as someone who had been crippled from birth. Why not use a stranger?

This was miraculous. I had never witnessed anything like this. I had certainly heard stories of this Galilean doing other amazing things, but

I just assumed they were exaggerations. We all know what happens when many people pass along stories. Each retelling adds embellishments until the original story is lost in the fantastical drama that has been created. But this was something I had seen with my own eyes. How could I process what I had witnessed?

As I was considering the import of the event, I noticed the restlessness of the people around me. It looked as though the outraged and somewhat humiliated Pharisees and scribes wanted to get out of the house as quickly as possible. They had obviously failed in their attempts to bait Jesus with difficult questions earlier. Now they were embarrassed by this uneducated carpenter because He was able to heal and obviously had more power than them. His healing of the young man was a sign of His connection with God, surely. The entire crowd was in awe of Him. The Pharisees would not let this insult go unpunished. I knew that for sure. It would not be long until they were standing before my husband asking for help in removing yet another upstart from our city. They would create some story, I was sure, that would implicate my husband as an inept leader. Finally, they would appeal to Caesar if they had to. Their hypocrisy was astounding. They did not honor Caesar, but they did not hesitate to use his power when it suited their purposes.

As they flounced out of the house, many in the crowd also left. Some wore stunned expressions. Others were talking as fast as they could, relating the details of the story to those who were outside and could not see what had happened. They were enjoying the attention of their listeners. There would be many such retellings of the story this very night inside every home of the surrounding area.

My feet seemed stuck to the hard-packed mud floor beneath them. I watched all of the movement and action around me as if I was in a trance. I am not sure what I was feeling. Somehow I had lost my maid in all of the commotion. As I started to look around for her, I sensed someone watching me. I instantly reached for my hood, hoping that I had not been recognized. Raising my head slowly, I realized that Jesus was looking directly at me. He had not moved. He remained standing below the opened tile roof. As His disciples worked to handle the animated crowd,

Jesus stood still and calm in the chaos around Him. I am not sure how to put into words what His look communicated to me.

Have you ever felt that someone spoke to you with his eyes? It sounds so silly even as I say that, but it is exactly how I felt in that moment. The din of the movement and conversation in the house faded, and I felt as loved and comforted as the healed man. Tears streamed down my cheeks. I did not know what was happening to me. Then Jesus smiled a radiant smile, at me. My words cannot describe His smile well enough for you to understand what it was like. All I can say is that it was like what every smile should be. Without a word spoken, Jesus made me feel safer and more significant than anyone ever had before.

As I bowed my head to wipe my tears, I was jostled from behind. A strong hand captured my elbow, and I was steered outside into the sunlight once again. Before I knew it, Elsa, my maid was back at my side, and we hurried back toward the safety of home. We did not speak for several minutes. I was too emotional. The events of the past hour swirled through my mind. Had it really only been about an hour? I felt something momentous had just taken place. My first thought was to run to my husband and tell him what I was feeling. But how could I do that without admitting I had left the security of our compound without my guards while dressed as a Hebrew? He would be horrified. I would have to endure one of his stern lectures again. Also, how could I explain what had happened between Jesus and me? I could not find the words to describe it to myself.

My mind was in turmoil. My emotions were tingling. I had never previously felt this way. Somehow, I must get back into the presence of Jesus to learn more about His teaching and about Him. I did not know how I could make this happen. I just knew that I needed to learn more.

In the following days, Elsa and I had many discussions. She told me details about the prophecy of the coming Jewish Messiah. We talked about the possibility that Jesus might be that Messiah.

You must understand that since my husband had been appointed prefect, there had been a few men who claimed to be the deliverers of the nation of Israel. They were dealt with easily enough. I did not want to think too long about what had happened to them, but I knew that my husband had gotten rid of them. He could not allow anyone to threaten the Roman nation. However, I had never heard stories of any of these men healing sicknesses or feeding thousands of hungry people. Jesus, as I had seen for myself, was able to perform miracles. Yet, He did not seem to do anything simply for the attention. He always focused more on loving the people around Him. He pointed people to God and invited His listeners to trust God and remember how much God had done to show His love for them. This made Him stand apart from the Pharisees who always preened for attention and honor amongst the people.

I began to look forward to my discussions with Elsa and found myself spending more time with her than I did with any of my friends.

Although I longed to see Jesus again, I was not prepared for our second meeting. It did not happen out in the town somewhere. My next encounter with Jesus happened right in my own home.

The Pharisees developed a plot to accuse and arrest Jesus. They carried out their evil scheme during the night, which was so clearly against their own laws. It was another example of their willingness to ignore their very own laws if it meant helping their cause.

After the arrest, they decided to dump the problem of Jesus into my husband's lap. Did they know that history would be so cruel to the one responsible for Jesus' death? They brought Jesus to my husband and made the case for His guilt.

Elsa was the one who rushed into my room and told me what was happening. I hurriedly made myself presentable. As I rushed toward the Presentation Room, I felt myself trembling. Upon entering, I was overwhelmed by what I saw. Jesus was there, standing alone in the center of the room. His wrists were tied in front of Him. He had obviously been mistreated. There were several large, nasty bruises forming on His swollen face. His outer garment was torn and dirty. In spite of this, He still looked regal. His presence filled the room. His accusers never got too close to Him as if they were afraid to do so. Even my husband was unwilling to look at Him for longer than a moment.

When I entered the room, I was captivated by Jesus' eyes, as I had been during our first meeting. However, there was such sorrow in them this time. Somehow I knew that He was not sad for Himself but instead for all of us, even for the pompous men who were accusing Him.

I was instantly reminded of my dream from the previous night. In my dream, I saw Jesus standing on a mountain. He was looking down upon a city and weeping. As I struggled to think of how to comfort Him, I became aware that He was weeping for me. I struggled to tell Him that I was fine and did not need His great concern. There was nothing that should cause Him such grief, but He did not hear me. I awoke feeling a deep sense of foreboding. Now here He stood completely silent, while His accusers ranted and demanded that my husband execute Him. What an awful situation. My husband could not afford a riot, which the leaders of the city threatened if he did not get rid of this rebel.

Honestly, at that moment there was not much about Jesus that I truly understood, but I was convinced my husband had to be very careful with this situation. I could almost believe that Jesus was a man sent from God. I was not sure if He really was God's Son, the Messiah, as Elsa claimed. But He was most definitely not a normal human man. No human I knew could do what He had done, what I had seen with my own eyes.

I walked to my husband's side and warned him against being forced to make a judgment about this man. I briefly told him of my dream and urged him to allow the Pharisees to take the responsibility for this ruling. If they wanted Jesus put to death, then they would have to carry out this harsh punishment themselves.

Pilate turned away from me and began questioning Jesus. "You have been brought to me because You have made outrageous claims. You call Yourself King of the Jews. Is that who You are?"

Jesus did not answer right away. Antipas and his host of followers quieted and gawked at Jesus, waiting for His answer. Finally He said quietly, "It is as you say."

At that, the members of Antipas's party started to yell accusations at Jesus along with many questions. Jesus stood as still as He had when the crippled man was lowered before Him. His calm was such a contrast to the heated oaths and exclamations of the city leaders. My husband was amazed, as was I, by Jesus' demeanor.

"Do You not want to answer Your accusers? Do You not have any defense?"

Once again, Jesus was silent. From my husband's expression, I could tell he was greatly perplexed. In all of his years as prefect, he had never seen such calm in an accused man. He turned away from Jesus and faced the ranting leaders.

"I find no fault in this man. He is innocent."

That statement brought more shouting. The leaders started to accuse my husband of allowing Jesus to try to overthrow Caesar. Pilate had previously experienced some trouble with the Roman leadership. Antipas knew my husband could not afford more unrest.

As he always did when upset, my husband grabbed the front of his robe. He paced back and forth in front of Jesus, looking at Him, studying Him. I knew he was searching for a solution to the situation, one that would satisfy Antipas and his cronies but would save Jesus' life. Antipas watched like an asp ready to strike if he did not like the answer he received. The others around him all waited for his signal to know how they should respond. What detestable men they were.

Suddenly, Pilate stood still. From his expression, I knew he had found a solution to the problem. With a last look at Jesus, he turned to Antipas. He offered to have Jesus whipped and then released. It was Passover, the one time each year when a prisoner of the crowd's choosing could be released. Surely, this would satisfy Antipas and his cronies. Surely, the crowd would call for Jesus' release. They had been following Him around the city in mobs, witnessing the miracles He performed, and listening to His words of love and wisdom.

We did not know how busy the Pharisees had been in convincing the people that Jesus should be crucified.

Pilate walked to the edge of the balcony to speak with the crowd gathered below. When Pilate offered to release Jesus, the crowd chanted a different name. "Barabbas. Give us Barabbas."

He was one of the most brutal men ever to live in the city. He was even responsible for the killings of two young children while robbing their parents. No one really knew how many other lives he had taken.

The entire city had breathed a sigh of relief when he was captured a few weeks earlier. Why would they cry for his release?

Pilate raised his arm to quiet the crowd and again forcefully stated that he could find no fault in Jesus. There was nothing for which to convict Him. Even before he finished speaking, Antipas had the rest of the leaders stirred into a frenzy. They engaged with the crowd from the balcony. The crowd continued to chant wildly, "Barabbas, Barabbas."

"What should I do with Jesus?" my husband asked.

The crowd roared, "Crucify Him. Crucify Him."

I was devastated. I did not know how to help my husband, how to save Jesus. The crowd would soon cause a riot. The priests and Pharisees must have planted instigators in the crowd. Surely, these people could not be so fickle as to follow Jesus one day and turn against Him the next.

I could tell the moment when my husband knew that he would have to sacrifice an innocent man to appease the city leaders and keep peace in the streets. He took a deep breath before speaking. "Bring me a bowl of water," he ordered a servant standing close by.

I had no idea what he was doing. When the servant returned, he bowed before Pilate offering him the bowl. Pilate took one last look at Jesus, and plunged both hands into the clear water. "I wash my hands of this Man's blood." As he turned toward Antipas and the others, he repeated, "I wash my hands of this Man's blood. I find no fault in Him. May His blood be on your hands."

Finally, he turned to the crowd still shouting up to us from below the patio. He raised his hands for silence. Water ran down his arms as he yelled one last time. "This Man has done nothing wrong. His blood be on your heads."

I think I was in shock at that point. No matter what Pilate said, he would certainly be blamed for this crucifixion. A part of me knew that history would not be kind to him. But what more could he do? How I wished in that moment that we had never come to Judea but remained on our quiet farm. How I wished that Pilate had never gotten involved in the government. There were so many wishes that flew through my mind in seconds. But none of them mattered.

As soon as Pilate lowered his arms, the guards grabbed for Jesus. They pulled Him forcefully from our presence. His expression did not waver even when one of the soldiers kicked Him to hurry Him along. My last impression of Him that day was that He was at peace in spite of the horrendous sentence, almost as if He knew what was going to happen and had already accepted His fate. I did not understand then how that could be possible.

After the city leaders left our house, my husband stood in the middle of the room. I wanted to comfort him, but did not know what to say. Several minutes passed with us both standing still. We could hear the noise of the mob and the loud cry the moment the soldiers emerged from the house with Jesus in their grasp. The crowd was hungry for blood. My only hope was that after the whipping torture Jesus was about to endure, the priests would relent and not follow through with the crucifixion. Even as I made that wish, I knew it would never happen that way.

I looked over at the doorway, just as my husband left the room. I was not sure what I should do. I felt lost. I could not erase the memory of the night before and the tears Jesus had wept for me in my dream. I wanted to weep for Him today. I felt helpless and hopeless.

Upon returning to my rooms, I saw Elsa, and she peppered me with questions. She was so distraught that I could not be angry with her.

"How can they do this to our Messiah? I do not understand," she wailed. "Isn't there anything the master can do to help Jesus?" In that moment, I wished I could give her the answer she wanted, the answer I wanted. Her grief was my grief. I gripped her hand, and we wept together.

Later that afternoon, I could no longer sit in my room. I had to take the risk to see Jesus one last time. It was dangerous, but I was overcome with grief. I had to try.

After I dressed again in the Hebrew costume, Elsa and I made our way out of the house and hurried to the barren area just outside the city where crucifixions took place. It was a small hill where refuse from the city was dumped. It was a place of stinking smells, burning garbage, and human waste. Desperately, I tried not to think about what I was about to witness. Although I knew of the practice of crucifixion, I had never seen it for myself. Many of my friends would travel on litters carried by their slaves to witness the horror. They found some kind of entertainment in the agony of others. Even the most evil men certainly did not deserve such cruelty.

As we approached Golgotha, I was almost overcome by the smell of death. It enveloped Elsa and me. We clutched each other's hands tightly in desperate fear. There were three crosses on the small hill ahead of us. Somehow, I knew that Jesus was the broken and mangled body hanging from the middle cross. My eyes were drawn to Him as my heart was drawn to Him from the first moment I saw Him standing in the lowly hovel that day not so long ago.

The crowd ignored the criminals on either side of the middle cross and shouted obscenities up at Jesus. They raised their fists and called Him names. The Roman soldiers worked diligently to keep them back from actually attacking Him as He hung helplessly on the wooden bars.

We were able to wedge our way through the angry mob of onlookers. Standing before the splintered wooden cross, we stared at the bloody body of Jesus, the man we thought was the Messiah of Israel. I felt numb with disbelief. My husband had allowed this to happen. He should have done more, risked his own life if necessary.

Blood seeped from the wounds in the dirty feet just an arm's reach away from my face. The large metal spike that held them in place was rusty and tilted left, as if the soldier who hammered it into place did not know how to weld a mallet. I was afraid to raise my eyes. I wanted to shut out all of the sights, sounds, and smells around me. But I was compelled to look up even though I was terrified to do so.

I could see His ribs pushing against ribbons of flesh as Jesus gasped for each breath. The whipping He received had been vicious. I could imagine what His back would look like. His chest was shredded from the leather straps that would have wrapped around with each lash from the muscled soldier assigned the gruesome job of scourging.

On Jesus' head, was a crude crown made of thorns. I could not believe what I was seeing. How could humanity be so heartless? The thorns had been driven into the swollen flesh. The face that once looked at me with so much love and compassion, was now misshapen beyond recognition. His eyes were closed. I was not sure they could be opened because of the horrible swelling of His battered face. If I had not heard the curses of those around me, I could have convinced myself that this was not Jesus. There was nothing recognizable about Him.

Then, somehow He opened His eyes. Those eyes. Jesus looked into my soul. And in that moment, I felt a peace. Peace in the midst of hell. Peace that passed what I could comprehend. I did not try to understand. I accepted.

With a great effort, He heaved His broken body up to gasp a breath.

"Father, forgive them. They do not know what they are doing."

I could not believe my ears. Jesus had just asked God to forgive those people who were crucifying Him, causing Him such pain, and cursing Him as He hung before them dying.

Before that thought was fully formed, I realized that I was one of those people who needed His forgiveness, too. The impact of that realization hit me, and I almos doubled over with the weight of it. Jesus did not deserve what was happening to Him, and yet He did not condemn us for what we were unjustly doing to Him.

At His words, the crowd quieted for a moment. The soldier at the foot of the cross paused and turned to gaze up at Him. His shoulders trembled. He took a half step forward and hesitated. It appeared as though he was about to speak when the criminal on the right side of Jesus cried out in anguish.

"Jesus, remember me when You come into Your kingdom." The man's voice was hoarse with pain. He could barely form the words, but in that one statement, there was hope. So much hope.

In the midst of the agony and suffering, this criminal's plea convinced me that Jesus truly was a king, the King. He was greater than Pilate, my husband, greater even than Caesar. He was the One able to forgive sin, to release us from guilt, to pardon us, and take us to heaven. Even as He hung on the wooden cross amidst the worst of humanity, His message of love and hope radiated.

"Today, you will be with Me in Paradise."

It was a gasped promise that brought peace to the man. It was a promise that brought hope into my own heart. The horror that surrounded me faded. I was captured once again by Jesus' eyes.

Once more, His chest heaved with the effort to take a single breath.

"Father, it is finished. Into Your hands I commit My spirit."

Those were the last words I heard from His lips. His head slumped forward. A darkness slowly built around us. Even though it was only midday, the sky continued to grow dark. The crowd stopped cackling and began to withdraw, awed by what was happening in the sky. The soldiers stood more alert.

Once again, the Roman soldier standing closest to the cross moved toward it a step. He raised his eyes to the limp human form held to the cross by three angry metal spikes. Whispering to himself, he mumbled, "Surely, this was a righteous man." I would not have heard him if I had not been so close.

Elsa's sobbing tore my gaze away from the form on the cross. I realized my face was wet with my own tears. Elsa grabbed my right arm and began to drag me away from the hill. "We must return home. There is a storm coming, the darkness..." I did not hear the rest of what she said. I do not remember the journey home. All I could think of were Jesus' words.

Father, forgive them.

Today you will be with Me in Paradise.

It is finished.

Into Your hands....

Those were words of such conviction. Words of such hope. Words of such peace. Words that I needed to hear.

I walked away from Golgotha that day a different woman. I was a woman who knew of forgiveness, hope and peace. My story continued, and I was never the same. Encountering Jesus and experiencing His love created a new life in me.

You knew the story of my husband, Pontius Pilate, or at least part of his story. Now you know a bit more about him and a small part of my story.

Perhaps you will be compelled to look into your own heart, to your own story, and begin to consider how to judge yourself. Who do you think Jesus is? Is He the King in your life, or do you wish to wash your hands of Him? Can you open your heart to receive His love, forgiveness, peace and hope?

My prayer is that you will be willing to reach out to Him as the thief on the cross did, and ask Him to bring you into His kingdom.

9

Chaviva

Unless you are very fond of historical reading, you will not find my name familiar. It is Chaviva. My brother was named James. I had several other siblings, but it is James's story that I want to tell. It is the story of an angry boy who became an angry man. It is the story of a boy who was always striving and working to earn his way and earn the love and recognition that were already his. It is the story of never being able to measure up, always feeling frustrated, and engaging in a power struggle. And because of God's amazing mercy, it is the story of a life converted by sacrifice and forgiveness.

From my earliest memories, James was always hardworking. Even though he was not the eldest in the family, he strived to be the one in charge. He studied hard and tried to perform better in school than any of us.

My father was a carpenter, and so all of my brothers grew up learning that trade. My oldest brother was a gifted carpenter. His first independent project will forever stand out in my memory. Even though it was just a simple stool for my mother, the craftsmanship was striking. Father brought it into the house with an astonished look on his face. He showed it to Mama, and with tears in his eyes, he whispered something to her. Even though I strained, I could not catch what he said. My mother put her hand on her heart and closed her eyes. She bowed her head for a moment.

When she opened her eyes, she looked at my father and paused before saying, "Joseph, how could it not be so beautiful. He is a natural creator. We should not be surprised by this ability."

I did not really understand what she meant by that statement at the time. However, I do remember a couple of things from that afternoon. One is that James, who was only nine at the time, became quite upset and ran out of the room. My oldest brother looked sad when James left but returned to the shop with Father right after that. We had that stool in our home for many years. It was a favorite of Mama's. In fact, it was one of the most beautiful pieces of furniture we owned.

James also tried to make a stool for our mother later that week. He always tried to out-work, out-do, out-perform his older brother. James's stool was made from the same wood, and it was what you might expect from the efforts of a young boy just learning the trade. The legs were a bit wobbly. Father made a big deal out of the presentation of James's stool. Mama clapped her hands and thanked James for his effort. James was not fooled. He could see with his own eyes that for all of his hard work, his stool did not measure up to the other.

This story illustrates James's entire life. He worked so fiercely hard. He always wanted to be the best, the one in charge. His entire life was a competition with his older brother.

He liked to be right and would argue incessantly to prove his point. All through the years when Father was still alive, I remember him gently taking James by the hand and leading him out to the workshop in the middle of arguments with one of us. It was his gentle way of intervening and bringing any unpleasantness to an end. Since Father was a man of few words, he never engaged in an argument started by James. After these times in the carpentry shop with Father, James would return, sullen and silent.

One memory that makes me chuckle now is remembering when James tried to scare away any young men who happened to show even the slightest interest in my sisters or me. He would appear from our father's carpentry shop carrying the biggest saw he could find. He would ask lots of questions while walking around the bewildered young man, slapping the saw in his palm loudly. Who would ever want to return to our house after that?

James had a permanent scowl on his face and a harsh word on his tongue. It seemed as though he could not help but argue with everyone about everything.

These arguments upset our mother quite a bit. The worst arguments were the ones that James picked with our eldest brother. After our father died, there was no one with the authority to force James to stop. The fighting and competition escalated. James was masterful at involving all of us in his chaos, even me on occasion.

As the oldest child in our family, my eldest brother had certain rights but also many responsibilities. One of the things I loved was the way confusing passages from the Holy Scriptures were explained using simple stories or illustrations from nature to help us understand. All of us, except James, loved these stories. My eldest brother would often entertain us with stories of talking animals and their adventures. He would use these stories to describe what heaven was like. Those were my favorite stories. Every time it was my turn to choose a tale for my big brother to tell, I would ask for stories of heaven. When I listened to them, I longed to be there. The sadness of leaving this world did not seem so great when compared with the joy of the place we would go to live next. These stories of heaven helped all of us after the death of our father.

As we all grew older, the competition James created for himself intensified. Although James had grown in his carpentry skills, our eldest brother was more talented and created the most beautiful furniture and farming implements, most of the time even better than our father's. He was able to bring such beauty from the wood. He enjoyed his time in Father's carpentry shop. He enjoyed creating things. Once when I asked how it was possible to make such a lovely, delicate doll for our youngest sister, Maura, the answer was simply stated.

"That little doll was only hiding within the wood. All I had to do was chip and sand away all the extra wood to reveal her waiting there for Maura to love."

James always tried to prove that he was equally as talented. He went so far as to go to some of the people in the village and offer his services at a lesser price to try and steal business away from the family shop. He waited until after Father's death to do this, as Father would never have allowed such a thing if he had still been alive.

I cannot remember one time when my brother baited or challenged James. He refused to be drawn into a verbal battle with James. His humble answers just seemed to agitate James even further. James's tongue was like a knife, cutting and wounding. No one in the family or in the village ever wanted to cross James.

Our eldest brother only showed anger when James happened to pick on one of us, or if he upset our mother. He would respond to James at these times with such erudite answers that James could not argue. There were many times when James left the house swearing and upset after being bested in some silly argument.

What was it in James that drove him to try to prove that he was better at everything than the rest of us? Why did he always argue about everything? He claimed that he loved God, but as he was told many times, what is in the heart of man flows out through his tongue and his actions. James's tongue could be very sharp toward all of us. None of us wanted to be on the receiving end of his attacks. When our eldest brother left our house and began a public ministry, James grew even angrier. By now you might have guessed the name of my eldest brother.

Jesus.

After He left home, there was hardly a meal when James was not complaining about what Jesus was doing. "He now travels with a group of rough fellows and women of highly questionable character, walking through the streets and stirring up all kinds of trouble. He has even decided to call Himself the Son of Man. Mother, we must do something about this. If our father was still alive, he would never have allowed this."

These outbursts greatly upset Mama. She tried to calm James, but no one could do that. I know that she was very concerned about the attention Jesus was drawing from the Pharisees. They were irate about His teaching and His claim that He could forgive sins. When James heard that our brother had made such a claim, he erupted in anger. He paced around the room, shouting and threatening. Finally in frustration, he lifted up the stool that Jesus had made years earlier, and threw it against the wall. It splintered into pieces.

"Perhaps if our dear brother would try working a bit harder to help support this family and Himself, then He would not get into so much trouble. He has lost His mind. He is going to cause trouble for this entire family, mark my words. Soon the Pharisees will be knocking on our door, demanding that we reign Him in."

As the weeks went by, James grew more and more agitated. Daily, he told stories of Jesus' escapades. He was mingling with and touching lepers, who then claimed to be healed and tried to re-enter their communities. He was eating and drinking with tax collectors, prostitutes, and other outcasts. He was bringing shame on our family.

Even though James had always been an angry person, he did seem to be making some sense in his complaints. Jesus' association with these people was bringing our family unpleasant attention. There was a lot of talk circulating including discussion about whether Jesus had gone mad or had been possessed by a demon. The Pharisees were becoming more and more upset with Jesus.

Finally, James had enough and rounded us all up, including. He decided we should find Jesus, restrain Him, and bring Him home. "We need to get Him away from this crowd of outcasts and talk some sense into Him. We cannot sit back and watch Him destroy Himself and our family name along with Him. It is our duty to stop Him before He ends up getting Himself arrested or worse."

It was terrifying to think of my strong, calm, loving brother being mad or demon-possessed. It was equally upsetting to think of Him being imprisoned by the Romans. James had all of us convinced by his passionate arguments that what we were about to do was best for Jesus.

The next morning we set off to find Jesus and bring Him home. All of us went along: Joses, Judas, Simon, my sisters, and even Mama. We were quite a group. When we arrived at the home where Jesus was teaching and receiving masses of sick people, we were shocked to see the huge crowds. So many people wanted to get near Him. We heard many conversations about Him as we waited in a long line to try to get inside the house and reach Jesus.

"Do you know He healed my cousin who had been blind since birth?" one young man asked his friend.

"My father had a crushed foot from an accident in his cart. He had not walked since he was young man. Jesus saw him one day as I was wheeling him to temple. My father asked nothing of Him. But Jesus stopped beside the cart, reached out His hand, and placed it on my father's ankle. Father moaned loudly. Later he described the moment as one of intense heat, almost unbearable. But when Jesus removed His hand, my father's foot and ankle were whole again. He jumped out of our little wooden cart and starting dancing and praising God right there in the street. I have never seen anything like it. I was so astonished at the sight of my father dancing, that I did not think to thank Jesus. That is why I am here today. I want the opportunity to say thank you."

These kinds of stories began to make me wonder what was happening with my brother. What was going on? I was not sure what to think. I just wanted things in our family to be normal again.

It was almost half an hour before we made it close enough to someone who appeared to be in charge. James was red in the face by this time and loudly demanded to see Jesus.

"Do you know who we are? This is Jesus' mother, and we are His brothers. Tell Him we are here to see Him and take Him home. We have been left standing out here for too long. Give Him this message immediately."

James caused quite a scene. The talking around us ceased as he yelled at the man, whose name we learned was Andrew. I thought I recognized him. He was a local fisherman. He was very patient to stand there and listen to my brother ranting for as long as he did. He politely told James he would take our message to Jesus, nodded to my mother, and disappeared inside the house.

It was not long before he returned. I could tell right away that the news was not going to please James or my other brothers. Andrew looked first at my mother before speaking.

"Jesus has sent you His greetings. He is happy to have you here so you can witness what God is doing for His people. However, He says to tell you that these people are His brothers and sisters. He says He cannot leave them. This is the purpose for which He was born." Andrew spoke the next words to my mother, directly. "Jesus said to tell you that He is about His Father's business."

When Andrew gave this final message, my mother inhaled sharply. James roared so loudly that the crowd pulled back from us. Now, who was causing a scene? I thought for one horrible moment that he was going to strike Andrew. Mama reached out and touched his arm.

"James, it is time for us to return home. Your brother is doing what He must do." Then quietly she whispered, "I knew this time would come."

James swore and shoved his way through the crowd, knocking one young child to the ground. Her parents lifted her up and yelled after him, but he did not stop to apologize. He left us to do that for him. I knew that Mama was embarrassed because I was, too.

We all were wondering what Jesus meant by His words. Was He no longer a part of this family? Our father had been a carpenter, so what did He mean by *His Father's business*. I could not wait to get home and talk with Mama. Of course, I did not want to think about the anger that we would have to endure when James arrived home.

Over the next several months, we rarely saw Jesus, but we continued to hear many stories about Him. He did come to visit us, occasionally. At those times, He would sit quietly with Mama. They looked to be in deep conversation together, and none of us interrupted them. Most of the time, Jesus would visit when James was not home.

Any time James spoke of Jesus, it was to complain. "Now He is claiming to be the Son of God. He has people actually believing this nonsense.
The Pharisees are tired of the chaos He is causing. This is not going to
end well. He is going to end up getting into serious trouble. He is going
to cause this family serious trouble."

We had no idea how much trouble Jesus was going to cause and what
would end up happening to Him.

Three years after Jesus started His public ministry, James's predic-
tions came true. Jesus ended up paying a terrible price for all of the
commotion He stirred up. The Pharisees manipulated the Roman government into crucifying my brother. Not one of us attended the awful
event. James forbid us to go. He was unsure whether we might be recognized as family and end up in trouble, also. He did not say anything in
front of our mother, but with us he repeated many times that Jesus had
brought this on Himself with His grandiose ideas and claims of divinity.

I know that Mother did secretly go to Golgotha to see Jesus, even
though she never said anything to any of us about it for several days.
However, later, it was a story we all listened to over again many times.

I was at home when John, one of Jesus' disciples, walked her home.
She was devastated and needed my help to get to bed. The next morning
she wanted to talk. She told me that as Jesus hung on the cross, He told
John to take care of her.

This made me so angry. We should have been there supporting our
mother, even if we did believe that Jesus had completely lost his mind.
One of my brothers should have escorted Mama to the awful place called
Golgotha. It was not safe for women to go there alone, especially the
mother of one of the criminals. James should have taken her. He was the
second born.

He had struggled all his life to best Jesus. He had always wanted to
be in charge in our home. He had argued for his way almost every day.
Where was he when he was needed, when it was his time to step into the
leadership of this family? The rage I felt as Mama spoke was fierce.

Even though James blamed Jesus for His death to all who would listen, I could not help but notice a change in him after the day of the

crucifixion. He was less argumentative for the two days following. He only spoke when asked a direct question. John and Andrew came by the house again Friday evening and had a long, private conversation with James. Andrew was the disciple who had turned us away that day so long ago when we tried to rescue Jesus from the crowds. That was pretty close to the beginning of this insanity. If only we had been able to convince Jesus to stop back then. He would probably still be alive.

During the time the three of them were talking that evening, I did not hear James raise his voice once.

If I had to put a name to the change I saw in him, I would say that James seemed less sure of himself and of everything else.

The days after the death of our oldest brother were filled with deep sadness and fear. We had lost our tender, loving brother. We were afraid that the Romans would now be watching the other men in our family to make sure that none of them would try to continue Jesus' ministry. On the evening of the third day after Jesus' death, Mother brought unbelievable news to us.

"Jesus has risen from the dead. His grave is empty. I have seen it for myself. Andrew took me there. Even the Roman guard posted at the tomb could not stop Him from doing what He said He would do. He is alive."

We all sat, silently staring at our mother. Part of me thought her mind had crumbled under the pressure and stress of losing her eldest son, but part of my mind began to remember some of the things Jesus told us throughout His life.

I waited for James to explode in anger, but for the first time ever, he remained silent. All of us were looking to him to handle this situation. Joses stared hard at him. When he continued to sit silently, Simon finally spoke on behalf of all of us. "Are you sure that Peter, the fisherman, did not simply steal the body and hide it? They could be trying to prolong this whole hoax."

Mother looked at Simon, joy streaming from her face. "Simon, James, all of you, listen to me. Jesus is really who He claimed to be. I know it is difficult to comprehend. He was your brother, but He is so much more than that. He is also your Savior, your God."

James jumped to his feet and rushed out of the room. I don't know where he went, but he did not return for a while. When I saw him again, he looked bedraggled, like he had not slept at all.

James looked rugged when he returned. Andrew was with him. I had never seen him like this. He did not smell very good either. As I looked at him, I noticed another unusual thing. He was calm. Maybe that sounds strange to say. But in all my years, I cannot remember once thinking that James looked calm. He was always on the move, always active, moving as if driven to do so, as if his life depended on being as busy as possible. He had a crease between his eyebrows even as a young boy. Now as I gazed at him, his face was relaxed, and there was something else there.

"Where have you been, James? We needed you here." There was so much more I wanted to say, but I was overcome with emotion: anger, grief, frustration. James reached out to me and did something he had never done in his entire life. He grabbed me and hugged me as though he would never let go. I was dumbstruck. I looked over at Andrew who was standing there smiling. Slowly, Andrew turned and left our home.

James was still holding me. I pushed against his grip a bit until he released me. When I was free, I stepped away so I could look at his face. There were tears in his eyes.

"James, what is going on? What is wrong with you?"

His answer was such a surprise. After he had motioned for me to sit, he told me an amazing story. I could never have guessed that I would have such a conversation with James.

James recounted being frantic after Jesus was arrested. He tried everything he could think of to rescue Jesus from the trouble He had caused for Himself. He spoke with anyone and everyone he knew who had any power. He had to get Jesus released.

"I tried every option I could think of, Chaviva. I was so angry with Him, but I did not want Him to die." James had to pause for a moment before continuing the story.

James was standing in the crowd when Pilate offered to release Jesus. Instead, the crowd cried out for the release of Barabbas, a local criminal. After that moment, he accepted that Jesus would really be killed because of His claims of being the Messiah.

"I ran away from Pilate's house and didn't stop until I thought my lungs would explode. I found myself in a vineyard."

He flung himself on the hard ground and wept. Hours passed and James remained there. He said that he must have fallen asleep, for the next thing he remembered was the sound of a rooster crowing to awaken a new day.

That was Friday. By the time James figured out where he was, it was already about mid-morning. Jesus was already on the cross.

"I was on my way home, Chaviva, when the sky suddenly darkened. Everyone around me was puzzled and fearful. No one knew what was happening. This had never happened before. I knew I should have done something to save Jesus, but I could not. All of my efforts were useless. I had failed to protect my brother from harm."

After returning later on Friday evening, James remained quiet and withdrawn. However, by Sunday, he confessed that he could not bear to listen to our mother as she tried to convince us that Jesus had risen from the dead. He was confused, heartsick, and guilty about not being able to save his brother. Once again he felt he must leave the house and find some answers.

"As I left, I saw Andrew. We spent that entire night talking about Jesus and what He had spent the last three years of His life doing. Andrew shared many stories and insights with me."

James had a difficult time believing what Andrew shared. But at the same time, he was not completely surprised. There had always been something different, unique, about Jesus. Maybe that is why he had always argued with Him and tried to pick fights.

By morning, Andrew almost had him believing that Jesus really was more than just a man. But if that was so, why did He end up on the cross?

"Surely the Messiah did not come to die on a Roman cross. And I could not accept the belief that Jesus could rise from the dead."

Andrew had not tried to fight with James. He had suggested instead that they pray and ask God to help James with his unbelief. That is just what they did. James spent the day with the disciples praying and talking. Just before dawn, this very morning, an amazing thing had happened.

"I awoke from the first peaceful night of sleep in almost three years to a soft light filling the area around me," James explained. "I was sleeping in the stable behind John's house. It took me a moment to realize the light was not the sunrise. It was completely silent, no roosters crowing the morning alarm. As I rubbed my eyes and sat up, a voice called my name. I knew that voice. It was the same voice that had urged me to have faith in my abilities as a carpenter whenever I became frustrated because my project was not turning out as well as His. That voice had reminded me that living a good life was more about loving God and others rather than working yourself to the bone.

It was Jesus' voice. I knew it.

Slowly, Jesus appeared right there before me. I cannot describe Him to you. He was the same and yet gloriously different. It was my brother's form but more than what He had been."

James paused again. He looked down at his clasped hands. When he looked at me again, he was smiling broadly.

"It's all true, my dear sister. Every word He spoke was the Truth."

Whatever happened that day, transformed James, forever. It erased all of the anger and embarrassment that James felt about his brother. All of James's protests and outbursts ceased. I never saw James argue again. His whole demeanor changed.

He became fast friends with John and Andrew. He spent hours discussing the last three years of Jesus' life with them. Before long, he was a leader in the group of disciples who met together weekly for prayer and encouragement.

In a few months, James became one of the teachers. It was not something I could ever have imagined. James, the arguer, now spoke about controlling the tongue. When he talked about the damage the tongue could do, I knew he was speaking from personal experience. He referred to the tongue as the rudder of a mighty ship.

"It is small," he would say, "but it can set the course of your life. It can bring strife and division, or if tended carefully, can bring life and healing."

He could tell people his own testimony of how submitting to Jesus could change a life from the inside out. He wrote down some of his teaching so that future generations would not forget the importance of a changed heart. He wanted people to know how important it was to experience a change in the soul, since that was the only way we could be transformed on the outside. He was able to describe the ugliness of bitter jealousy and selfish ambition and how they could destroy life. I knew he was remembering all of those moments from our childhood when he fought and argued with all of us, but especially with Jesus.

He encouraged us to allow our lives to be ruled by love for God and care for the needy, those whom he had called the rabble or the outcasts when Jesus was alive. He spoke about the fact that if the heart was truly changed, then cursing and blessing could not flow from the same mouth.

"Does a spring pour forth both fresh and salt water, or does a fig tree also produce olives? So, if our hearts are truly pure, then only mercy, peace and righteousness should flow forth. There should be no partiality or arguing among those of us who are followers of Jesus Christ our Lord. Look at the actions of your brothers and sisters. Where there is purity in their daily living, there is purity of heart. Without the fruit, the tree itself is dead, no matter how much it argues that it is alive."

Sometimes I wanted to pinch myself to see if I was dreaming when I heard James speak. He was sounding more and more like Jesus each day. His fame and importance were spreading. My brothers and sisters were convinced by his changed life that the message of Jesus was really the truth. He was the Messiah of Israel. We grew up with Him and did not believe Him. How could we have been so blind? I will never know.

James spent hours on his knees praying for the people sent out by the church in Jerusalem to share the gospel with others. He prayed for forgiveness for the people, asking God to soften their hearts in order that they might receive this good news of Jesus the Savior. Because of his devotion and desire for holy living, he became known as *James the Righteous* or sometimes as *James the Just*.

Now we had another famous brother in our family.

James was so radically different from the person we had known. He was very soft-spoken, which it took me a long time to accept. For at least two years, I found myself waiting for the old eruption of anger to come.

The Pharisees seemed to have a great respect for James. He often met with them to answer questions and explain the teachings of Jesus' followers. He also set up systems to take care of many of the orphans and widows in the city. The Pharisees liked this as it took the burden from their shoulders. He was always respectful, and I never thought that they would turn against him as they did.

However, the betrayal did come. Thankfully, it did not happen until after the death of our mother.

John had recently been banished to the Isle of Patmos when the soldiers showed up for James late one night. It was an advantageous time as most people were asleep, and so there were fewer people to protest the unlawful arrest and lack of a trial. In spite of the protests of some of the Pharisees, Ananus, the high priest, condemned James to be stoned to death. When I heard the sentence, I waited for an outburst from James. But there was none. He bowed his head for a moment. When he lifted his face and looked over at his family, there was a sad smile on his face.

"Do not be afraid my brothers and sisters. I will, today, be with our brother, Jesus. I am not afraid. Remember what He taught you from the beginning. Remember to love. Allow the love of God to transform your hearts and to form in you a new creation. Allow His Spirit to flow through you. Reach out to the needy around you. Truly, I will see you soon again."

Those were the last words spoken by my beloved brother, James.

10

Mary

At twelve years old, I thought I knew what my future held. I would be married to Joseph, a young carpenter from my village. I would live quite close by, and have a similar life to that of my mother. I admit that I was not really prepared for what was actually to happen. Nothing could ever have prepared me for the ultimate test I was about to face. It would stretch my belief and trust far beyond what I ever thought I could endure. But I was to learn that God's strength is made perfect in weakness and that His grace is sufficient in absolutely every situation He allows us to experience. I could never have anticipated the joy, honor, excitement and privilege, or the shame, humiliation and sorrow. I don't think anyone could have been prepared for that.

Growing up in a close Jewish family, I knew that I was loved. Our parents taught us about God and His commandments. Our heritage as God's people was something that was important to us in our everyday lives. We were careful to follow the teachings we heard in synagogue each week and did so out of gratitude and love for God, not merely from obligation. Even though I followed all of the Jewish teachings, I always had questions. Many times, the answers given to me were not satisfying. However, the one answer that really mattered proved to be deeply satisfying, but the cost of learning that answer was far beyond what I could ever have imagined.

I'm sure that many of you know about me. At least you know who I am when you hear my name: Mary, Jesus' mother. There is so much in that title. You know I was engaged to Joseph when Gabriel, the angel, visited me. But let me tell you a bit more background to my story.

Certainly, my family had heard descriptions of what angels looked like from the Holy Scriptures while attending synagogue. My friends and I had sometimes joked about what it would be like to see such a sight. Some of the holy writings described beings with eyes on all sides of their heads, wings like eagles, and faces like lions. We often thought we might fall to the ground and never stand again if we ever beheld such a sight. I did not realize at the time that I would have the chance to see an angel for myself very soon.

One day while cooking with Mama, she told me something surprising. Actually, when she first spoke, I thought she was joking with me. Let me explain myself. Sometimes when helping Mama cook, I would daydream, and one of the ways she would get my attention was to say something so outrageous, it would capture my wondering mind.

"Cousin Elizabeth is with child."

That short statement was shocking. Both Elizabeth and her husband Eli were quite old and well beyond childbearing years. Elizabeth had prayed for children faithfully ever since she first married, long before I was born. Since she had never been blessed with any children of her own, she had taken a great interest in me. She was definitely my favorite cousin. Since she was closer to my mother's age, I viewed her as an aunt and sought her wisdom on many topics. I often visited her and enjoyed the many conversations and laughs we shared. She was always so patient with my endless questions. She did not scold me like my father did and call me "The Question Queen". Now she was finally going to be a mother. It was almost unbelievable. I could not wait to visit Elizabeth and ask her about the visit from the angel that Eli claimed to have experienced.

What did the angelic being look like? Did he have a deep voice when he spoke? Was it terrifying? Did he shine? Were there wings? The questions exploded in my mind.

Elizabeth's story reminded me of one of my favorite stories from the Holy Scriptures, the story of Hannah. It was a story I always enjoyed hearing. I often found myself wondering what feelings Hannah must have had when she found out she was actually pregnant after praying for a child for so long. She had promised to give her child back to God if she, in fact, did conceive. The story in the Scriptures did not elaborate on her feelings as she took her young son, Samuel, to be raised by the priest.

How did she walk away and leave him there? How very painful it must have been. Did Samuel cry for his mother? How did she deal with her loneliness? I asked all of these questions and many others every time my father recited that story. He would patiently try his best to explain that we did not really know, as there was no more detail written down.

"Mary, you are too fanciful. Hannah simply did what she had to do. You need to accept this." No matter what he said, I continued to wonder about Hannah and her son, Samuel. Samuel was a well-known hero of our faith. Was there ever a greater prophet in our country? I always wished I could be as faithful and courageous as Hannah and Samuel. I had many times wished I, too, could one day hear God's voice calling to me as Samuel had from the time he was a young boy. Would I be able to answer as young Samuel had?

"Speak Lord, for Your servant is listening."

How could I ever guess that I would have the chance to experience some of the same feelings as Hannah when she had to let her son go and give him back to God? How could I know that God would give me a chance to answer His call just like Samuel?

My call from God came not too many weeks after hearing about Elizabeth. At the age of 13, I was formally betrothed to Joseph. He was a carpenter, a simple man you might say. He was strong from the work he did with his father in their wood shop and so handsome. He did not talk very much. He was more comfortable around logs and sawdust than around people. Our families were dear friends, and everyone was delighted with our betrothal. I was so excited to become Joseph's wife. We had been friends for all our lives. We enjoyed each other's company.

I have to confess that I did most of the talking when we were together. I would bring all of my questions to Joseph. Even though he often did not offer answers, he seemed content to let me ramble on. He listened and smiled at me. When he did speak, he reminded me of some wise saying from our religious teaching. He always made me feel safe, understood, and accepted. His quietness never bothered me. In fact, I think it helped me to settle down and not feel so agitated about the answers I felt I needed in life. Even though Joseph didn't have much money, I knew he would work hard to take good care of me. He was a God-fearing man of integrity. I was so thankful for that.

It was an ordinary day not long after our betrothal when my life changed forever. I guess having a visit from an angel does have an impact. I was sitting alone in one of my favorite spots not far from my home. If I finished my chores early, I would hurry to the tiny hill that was covered with olive trees, just about a five-minute walk from my house. It was usually quiet and cool. I could pretend that I was the only person alive there as it was completely deserted. I spent many hours thinking about answers to my abounding questions there. That day, I had been sitting quietly under a tree covered in plump olives, wondering again about Samuel, and trying to picture what he must have looked like when the air around me shimmered.

I rubbed my eyes thinking I must have dozed off for a moment. But, yes, the air was still shimmering almost as if there was silver and gold dust swirling before my eyes. Slowly, quietly, the form of a man appeared. He was taller than any of the men I had ever met. Although I could not really describe what he was wearing, I had the sense that he was a warrior. I have been asked time and again how I knew this. Did he hold a shield? Did he carry weapons? I cannot answer, but for some reason, I am convinced that he was a warrior. His entire form glowed brightly, as though he was covered in metallic dust. His face was radiant, joyful, and more than handsome, although I could not describe individual features. His entire being was captivating. I cannot find another word for it. I was so drawn to him but terrified at the same time. It was as if there was a force that drew me to him. I was completely overwhelmed. I wanted to yell, laugh, and cry all at the same time. I tried to speak but could barely move my mouth. I felt frozen to the trunk of the tree at my back.

The warrior spoke. "Greetings, you who are highly favored. The Lord is with you." He bowed before me. What did his words mean? I was just a normal girl, and no one considered me highly favored. I was the simple daughter of Jewish parents. I was more than puzzled by his words and still terrified. This must be a dream.

"Do not be afraid, Mary; you have found favor with God. You will conceive and give birth to a Son, and you are to call Him Jesus. He will be great and will be called the Son of the Most High. The Lord God will give Him the throne of His father David, and He will reign over Jacob's descendants forever; His kingdom will never end."

My thoughts were racing. I would conceive. I would conceive? A child? I did not understand how this could be.

I guess my chronic curiosity got the better of me, and I blurted out, "How can this be since I am a virgin?"

My father would have been horrified that I had the presumption to question someone obviously as important as this being before me. I could not stop asking questions, even in the synagogue when women were not supposed to speak. My parents would catch me mumbling them under my breath. Why could the teachers not answer our questions or explain things more fully?

When I realized I had spoken this question aloud, I covered my mouth with my hands. I waited for the warrior to roar his displeasure. He did not. He smiled. I felt my body relax a bit. I no longer felt quite so terrified. I realized that I was not imagining this. It was happening.

Surely, this must be an angel of God. As that thought crossed my mind, I looked into his face. He nodded ever so slightly and smiled as if in answer to my thoughts. His name was whispered into my consciousness—Gabriel.

Then Gabriel spoke aloud, "The Holy Spirit will come on you, and the power of the Most High will overshadow you. So the holy One to be born will be called the Son of God." As he spoke those words, he bowed his head, and there was an awesome reverence in his tone. He paused, then raised his face to the sky before continuing.

"Even Elizabeth your relative is going to have a child in her old age; she who was said to be unable to conceive is in her sixth month. For no word from God will ever fail." The last sentence was stated with such conviction that I felt myself shudder. Gabriel's eyes blazed. "God's word will never fail." His voice thundered. His body vibrated with radiance. He stared at me. I was mesmerized.

I heard my voice answering, "I am the Lord's servant. May your word to me be fulfilled."

I could hardly believe my own ears. It was as if my heart spoke without the help of my mouth. Gabriel appeared to grow larger and brighter at my words. A sound emanated from his chest. Was it laughter? That is what it seemed to be but purer and richer than any laughter I had previously heard. As it grew louder still, his form began to fade as he bowed his head to me. The silver and gold faded, and the surrounding countryside seemed terribly drab and colorless in contrast.

I do not know how long I sat there before I even thought about moving and returning home. Both my mind and body felt numb but energized. I kept repeating Gabriel's words and reliving the astonishment. Could this really be happening to me? Even knowing the prophesy about the Messiah and His birth, I could not fathom how this was really possible.

As I sat there under that olive tree, another thought came into my overwhelmed mind. I must go to see Elizabeth. I was so sure that this was what I needed to do. This thought got me up on my feet, and I ran faster than I thought possible back to my house.

Over the next couple of days, I told and retold the story to my parents many times. They were skeptical as you can expect. It was a fantastical story. Even though telling them was challenging, telling Joseph about Gabriel's visit was much more difficult. When I first came to him and told him that I was going to have a child, he was shocked. He was speechless, and the disappointment on his face was stark. He looked at me with great hurt in his eyes. I knew what he was thinking. He thought

I had betrayed our vows and been with another man. I tried to explain to him what had happened, but he silenced my quiet words with a single statement.

"Mary, you have broken my heart."

My voice simply would not work after that. Silence hung between us for many moments. As I bowed my head, I heard Joseph groan then dash out of the wood shop. Later that evening, he came by the house as he often did. As we sat quietly together with my parents not far away, he spoke. "I do not want to bring shame to you or your family, so I will divorce you quietly. I will keep your secret, Mary." He stayed only long enough to tell me that. Joseph's pain was the most difficult thing I had ever endured, his rejection, his brokenness. I felt like I had failed him, somehow. But that was only the beginning of my challenges.

If you remember the story, you know that God was gracious to me and sent an angel to Joseph to reassure him that the child I was carrying was who I had claimed: the Son of God, the Messiah. I am not completely sure of the conversation between Joseph and the angel because, as I said before, Joseph is not much of a talker. All I know is that the next time I saw Joseph, he was more excited than I had ever seen him. He rushed into our house, and without even speaking to my father, grabbed me and hugged me though my parents were standing there watching us. I knew my father was ready to step between us when he loudly cleared his throat. Joseph and I just laughed joyfully. It was so good to know that he understood what was happening to me and would once again be my biggest supporter and best friend.

Joseph and my family believed me, but just imagine living in a small town, and suddenly everyone finds out that you are pregnant and not married. For a while everywhere I went, people would stare and whisper, giggle. Some of my childhood friends avoided me. It was difficult. I was so young and overwhelmed. My parents decided to send me to stay with Elizabeth for a few months. I was eager to get away and have the chance to talk with Elizabeth. I still had the overwhelming feeling that I needed to see her. I needed to share my story with her. Somehow, I knew she would understand and encourage me.

Even though there is so much more I could tell you about those nine months before Jesus was born, I will try to continue on with the point of my story. Yes, I was Jesus' mother. It was a joy. No nagging, no disciplining, no correcting. But there were so many questions, so many moments that I wondered about the future. What was going to happen to my son, God's Son? What was it going to look like when He had to be *a lamb slain for the sins of His people*? What about the prophecy of His death in the prophet Isaiah's writing: *by His strips we are healed*. What would that mean for Jesus? I asked myself many questions over the 30 years that Jesus was with me. I stored up questions and moments in my heart. One day I hoped I would have answers. One day it would all become clear.

When that fateful day arrived, I was not ready for it. What can I say? It was beyond what words could describe: the pain, the suffering.

It was horrifying to see my son's body, bloodied, broken, abused and crucified. This was the child that Gabriel told me was the Son of God. He had always been so kind and caring to His brothers and sisters. He had obeyed all of our commands, served His family, and never complained. This was the little boy who could argue with the teachers of the law at the age of ten, who was determined and confident, but also humble and gracious. This was my firstborn son. The child I had delivered while still a virgin, frightened and alone in a strange town far from my family.

"Jesus, my son, what have they done to You?" I cried in agony as I stood at the foot of the Roman cross upon which He hung.

But the horror of His physical appearance was not as wrenching as the agony I saw on His face as He uttered some of His final words. At last, He heaved His destroyed form up to cry out in anguish, "My God, My God, why have You forsaken Me?"

Those words still ring in my ears to this day. I am not sure I would have recognized His voice. It was hoarse and ragged. His shoulders shook as a shudder of pain raced through His battered body. Jesus, who had always been the One reminding all of us of God's love, now felt abandoned by that same God. How could that be? What had He done that was so awful? How could the Father turn His back on His Son in so great a time of need?

I was horrified, devastated, and deeply weary. This was a nightmare. For the first time ever, I saw abject horror and abandonment in my child's face.

John, who was one of Jesus' disciples, stepped closer to me as I sobbed and fell to my knees. He took me by the arm and carried me away quickly from the horror of my dead son. I do not remember much about that afternoon other than the fact that the sky turned dark. The earth shook violently. And it was finished. Jesus' life ended.

It was not until early the following morning that the answers to my painful questions begin to fill my mind. The teachings about the Messiah of Israel swirled through my mind, as I lay half-awake after a tormented night. As each Scripture came to mind, a small ray of light leaked into my soul. The horrible vision of Jesus suffering the humiliation of crucifixion began to fade. I envisioned my son standing before me explaining the need for His sacrifice.

I remembered the first time He had done this. He was ten years old, and we thought we had lost Him on one of our journeys to Jerusalem. After checking through the entire group of families looking for Him, Joseph and I found Jesus back at the temple instructing the teachers of the law from the Holy Scriptures. The teachers were listening attentively to His explanations of mysteries, accepting what He was telling them. It was funny at the time to witness their expressions of shock, awe, and disbelief. No one had ever taught with such confidence, certainly no one as young as Jesus.

The meaning of the sinister events that had just taken place began to make sense to me. The prophecy was being fulfilled. Jesus' words drifted into my consciousness. It was as if He was right by my bedside speaking to me.

Remember the prophecies, Mother. This is why I was born.

The words from the prophet Isaiah came to mind.

But He was pierced for our transgressions, He was crushed for our iniquities; the punishment that brought us peace was on Him, and by His wounds we are healed. We all, like sheep, have gone astray, each of us has turned to our own way; and the LORD has laid on Him the iniquity of us all…. though He had done no violence, Yet it was the LORD's will to crush Him and cause Him to suffer, ...and though the LORD makes His life an offering for sin, After He has suffered, He will see the light of life and be satisfied...

Those words answered the questions I had screamed at God just yesterday standing at the foot of my son's cross. Jesus was the Son of God. He was born to be the sacrifice for the sins of mankind, the sacrifice for my sin. He had always known what He must do, who He was. Honestly, I had known too. Hadn't Gabriel told me that day beneath the olive tree? I had known it throughout Jesus' childhood. He was no ordinary human son. As His mother, I just hoped that somehow, the sacrifice spoken of in the Scriptures did not really mean Jesus' death. But in the early hours of that morning, the truth exploded in my mind.

That day my son became my Savior. For the first time I really understood the gravity of my sin. My Son was separated from His Father and experienced the shame and humiliation of a tortuous death for me. What love, what sacrifice!

After He has suffered, He will see the light of life and be satisfied...

Those words of the prophecy drifted across my mind again like a whisper.

...the light of life...

Jesus had spoken of being raised from the dead and seeing us again. All of us had thought that He was speaking in one of His parables, but could He really have been talking about actually coming back from the death of crucifixion? That question jolted me out of bed. I needed to talk to John. We needed to check the tomb.

Just a few short hours later, John and I were on our way to the tomb where my son's body lay. John had informed me that the women had taken care of wrapping Him with cloths and spices for burial. I had wrapped Him in cloths shortly after His birth. I should have wrapped Him after His death, but I was too distraught.

As we entered the desolate area where the burial cave was located, we were greeted by a large group of Roman soldiers. Some of them were standing directly in front of the large, smooth boulder that covered the mouth of the cave. Several others were off to the sides, chatting and laughing. As they heard our footfalls, they raised their weapons.

I reached for John's strong arm. Why would a guard be posted here? John motioned for me to stay where I was. He slowly approached one of the soldiers. They spoke in hushed tones for several minutes. When he returned to my side, he gripped my elbow and steered me back towards home. It was not until we were about halfway home that he told me what was happening.

Apparently, the Jewish leaders remembered Jesus claiming that He would be raised from the dead. They thought that perhaps His disciples would try to hide the body and make the claim that Jesus was in fact resurrected. They were trying to crush any rumors that might possibly continue to cause them problems. They wanted to stamp out the name Jesus once and for all time.

That day felt long and painful. Sabbath had always been a joy in our home. This Sabbath was filled with sorrow, questions, and a longing to see if Jesus' words meant what my heart hoped they did.

On the third day, I will rise.

Tomorrow was the third day. That thought filled my head all day and all night. Again, the night passed slowly. I was anxious to see the dawn of the third day, Sunday.

Just as the black of night slowly began to change to the early gray of morning, I rose and quickly dressed. All of the disciples were going to meet at Salome's house to pray and encourage one another. I could not wait to gather and ask Peter what he thought about the ideas that were bubbling through my mind. Maybe Andrew would have some insight.

It was not long into our gathering time, when we heard a knock at the door. We held our breath. Had the soldiers finally come to arrest the rest of the disciples, especially the men who had been with Jesus when He was arrested? The knocking turned to banging and yelling. Andrew crept over to the window that looked down on the front door. One of the women from our group was frantically banging on the outside door. Andrew nodded to Philip who raced down to open the latched door. When she was admitted into the room, she was smiling broadly and babbling so wildly that we could not understand exactly what she was saying.

"He is risen. I saw glowing men...angels. They said He has risen!"

My heart hammered joyously in my chest till I could hardly catch my breath. Her words caused hope to explode in me. Peter exploded, but with anger. His words were rash as he chastised Joanna for being ridiculous. Her words seemed so unbelievable to almost all in attendance. As a silence settled in the room after Peter's outburst, all eyes eventually settled on me. Were they all waiting for me to chastise Joanna also?

She stood in the middle of the room with her head held high. The look of joy on her face never faded, not even after Peter's gruff words. She stood her ground. Her eyes turned to me, and her smile broadened. I knew she spoke the truth. Jesus, my son, lived. The prophecy was fulfilled.

My heart accepted what my brain could barely grasp. I turned to look at Peter, then at John. I did not even need to speak. As I looked from one face to the other, I could tell the moment when they too remembered Jesus' words. They looked at each other. A moment later they were racing for the door. They rushed out of the house as if it were on fire. I knew their hearts were burning with hope as mine was. I called for Andrew. I, also, wanted to get to the tomb, to see with my own eyes what Joanna and the other women had seen, an empty tomb. Even though my mind and heart were racing, my feet steadily carried me towards the cave that acted as my son's tomb. By the time we arrived, Peter and John were standing just outside the open mouth of the cave. Where were the Roman guards who had been there just hours ago? Not one of them was still here.

Peter spoke first. "He is not here. His grave clothes are there, but His body is gone." He paused. He turned and looked at me. He spun toward John. His shoulders started to vibrate. His laugh boomed out. Peter was always loud and bold. Laughter filled the desolate area. It was so contagious that soon all of us were laughing.

Jesus was alive. Even the Roman guard could not stop that stone from rolling away. He had risen, just as He said He would.

Any lingering sorrow from just two days ago was forgotten in that moment. My laughter brought healing into my heart, joy and healing.

You will give birth to a son and you are to call him Jesus. He will be great and will be called the Son of the Most High. The Lord God will give Him the throne of His father David, and He will reign over Jacob's descendants forever; His kingdom will never end...

The words that Gabriel had spoken over 30 years ago floated back into my mind. *His kingdom will never end...*

Jesus was my son, but only for a short while here on earth. More importantly, He is God's Son. He came to die for the sins of the world. He willingly took my place on the cross, your place on the cross. He loved us enough to die in our place. He died for Peter, for John, for you.

Finally, I had no more questions to ask. I had all of the answers to my questions. I knew now why Jesus came. What His mission was. Who He really was. Why He had to die. I knew He was no longer dead but had risen. One day upon my death, I would see Him again. He would no longer be my son, but my Savior. It would be a sweet reunion. I had confidence about the future.

If only my father had been alive to see his Question Queen with not one question left to ask.

 Gina Bolton grew up on the island of Barbados in the West Indies. A leader of women's studies for the last 30 years, Gina makes her home in Pennsylvania where she teaches in public school. She is married and has two beautiful daughters.

Made in the USA
San Bernardino, CA
26 August 2016